Let's Keep in Touch

Follow Us   Online

Visit US at

www.learnpersianonline.com

f www.facebook.com/PersiaClubCo

 www.twitter.com/PersiaClub

Call

1-469-230-3605

 www.instagram.com/LearnPersianOnline

Online Persian Lessons Via Skype

It's easy! Here's how it works.

1- Request a FREE introductory session.

2- Meet a Persian tutor online via Skype.

3- Start speaking Real Persian in Minutes.

Send Email to: **info@LearnPersianOnline.com**

Or Call: **+1-469-230-3605**

www.learnpersianonline.com

... So Much More Online!

- **FREE Farsi lessons**

- **More Farsi learning books!**

- **Online Farsi – English Dictionary**

- **Online Farsi Tutors**

Looking for an Online Farsi Tutor?

Call us at: 001-469-230-3605

Send email to: Info@learnpersianonline.com

1,000 Most Common Farsi Phrases

Essential Expressions for Communicating in Farsi

By

Reza Nazari

& Mehdi Parvin

Copyright © 2017

Reza Nazari, Mehdi Parvin

All rights reserved. No part of this publication may be reproduced, stored in a retrieval system, or transmitted in any form or by any means, electronic, mechanical, photocopying, recording, scanning, or otherwise, except as permitted under Section 107 or 108 of the 1976 United States Copyright Ac, without permission of the author.

All inquiries should be addressed to:

info@learnpersianonline.com

www.learnpersianonline.com

ISBN-13: 978-1981704910

ISBN-10: 1981704914

Published by: Learn Persian Online Website

www.learnpersianonline.com

About Learn Persian Online Website

The *"Learn Persian Online Website"* was founded on the belief that everyone interested in Persian language should have the opportunity to learn it!

Established in 2012, the *"Learn Persian Online Website"* creates international opportunities for all people interested in Persian language and culture and builds trust between them. We believe in this cultural relations!

If you want to learn more about Persian, this beautiful language and culture, *"Learn Persian Online Website"* is your best starting point. Our highly qualified Persian experts can help you connect to Persian culture and gain confidence you need to communicate effectively in Persian.

Over the past few years, our professional instructors, unique online resources and publications have helped thousands of Persian learners and students improve their language skills. As a result, these students have gained their goals faster. We love celebrating those victories with our students.

Please view our website at:

www.learnpersianonline.com

About the Author

Reza Nazari is a Persian author. He has published more than 50 Persian learning books including:

- Learn To Speak Persian Fast series,
- Farsi Grammar in Use series,
- Persia Club Dictionary Farsi – English,
- Essential Farsi Idioms,
- Farsi Verbs Dictionary
- Read and Write Persian Language in 7 Days
- Laugh and Learn Farsi: Mulla Nasreddin Tales For Intermediate to Advanced Persian Learners
- Top 50 Persian Poems of All Time
- Farsi Reading: Improve your reading skill and discover the art, culture and history of Iran
- and many more ...

Reza is also a professional Farsi teacher. Over the past eight years, his online Persian lessons have helped thousands of Persian learners and students around the world improve their language skills effectively.

To participate in online Persian classes or ask questions about learning Persian, you can contact Reza via email at:

reza@learnpersianonline.com or his Skype ID: rezanazari1

Find Reza's professional profile at:

www.learnpersianonline.com/farsi-tutor-reza

Contents

Description 15
Pronunciation 16
Greeting 19
Thank You 20
Answer to Thank you 21
To apologize 22
Answer to apologize 23
Introducing 24
To Love 25
Like and dislike 26
To Agree 27
To Disagree 28
To Ask Questions 29
Understanding and lack of Understanding 30
Family 31
Clarification and Understanding 32
Making a Complaint 33
To Accept or To Refuse a Complaint 34
To Forget and To Remember 35
Fatigue 36
To Wait 37
Being Happy and Sad 38
Blaming and Refusing Blaming 39
Watching TV 40
To Help 41
Party 42
To Invite 43
Accepting Invitation 44

Refusing Invitation	45
Certainty	46
Uncertainty	47
To Request	48
Feelings and Blessing	49
To be Shocked	50
To Praise	51
The Weather	52
Time & Date	53
Warning	54
Expression of Opinions	55
Marriage	56
Apartment / House	57
Feelings	58
Making Offers	59
Making requests	60
Refusing Requests and Accepting Requests	61
Accepting Offers and Refusing Offers	62
Job	63
Future	64
News	65
Giving bad news and Responding to Bad News	66
Describing Personality	67
To Give Address	68
Sleep	69
Taxi	70
Complements	71
Making and Answering A Phone Call	72
Age	73

Promises and Useful Responses..74

Speaking in Farsi..75

Asking for Opinions 76

Hope and Disappointment..77

Health and Illness 78

Shopping 79

Booking 80

Description

Designed as a quick reference and study guide, this book offers guidance for situations including greeting, traveling, accommodations, healthcare, emergencies and other common circumstances. A phonetic pronunciation accompanies each phrase and word.

1000 Most Common Farsi Phrases is designed to teach the essentials of Farsi quickly and effectively. The common words and phrases are organized to enable the reader to handle day to day situations. The book should suit anyone who needs to get to grips quickly with Farsi, such as tourists and business travelers.

The book "1000 Most Common Farsi Phrases" is incredibly useful for those who want to learn Farsi language quickly and efficiently.

You'll be surprised how fast you master the first steps in learning Farsi, this beautiful language!

Ideal for self-study as well as for classroom usage.

Pronunciation

The regular letters used for written Persian stand for some different sounds. It is usually difficult to tell how a word is pronounced just by looking at how it is spelled. Therefore, it is useful to show the pronunciation of each word separately, using a system of symbols in which each symbol stands for one sound only. The pronunciations of letters and words are given within two slashes. This book uses a simple spelling system to show how letters and words are pronounced, using the symbols listed below.

Symbol	Example	Symbol	Example
a	hat /hat	m	move /muv
â	cut / cât	n	need /nid
âi	time /tâim	o	gorgeous /gorjes
ch	church /church	ô	coat/ côt
d	dog /dâg	u	mood /mud
e	men /men	p	park /park
ei	name /neim	r	rise /râiz
f	free /fri	s	seven /seven
g	get /get	n	nation /neishen
h	his /hiz	t	train /treyn
i	feet /fit	v	vary /vari
iyu	cute /kiyut	y	yet /yet
j	jeans /jinz	z	zipper /zipper
k	key /ki	zh	measure /mezher/
kh	loch /lakh	'	sounds like a slight pause between two letters.
l	loss /lâs	sh	shoes/shuz
gh	sound "r" in French word "Paris"		

Greeting		احوالپرسی
		ahvâlporsi
English	Pronunciation	Persian
Hello!	salâm	سلام!
How are you?	chetori?	چطوری؟
How are you doing?	hâletun chetore?	حالتون چطوره؟
I'm fine!	khubam.	خوبم!
Not too bad!	bad nistam	بد نیستم!
How are doing?	chikar mikoni?	چیکار می کنی؟
What's up?	che khabar?	چه خبر؟
Everything's good!	salâmati	سلامتی
Tanks god!	khodâro shokr.	خدا رو شکر
Is everything's alright?	hamechi khoobe?	همه چی خوبه؟
How's your family?	khunevâdat chetoran?	خونوادت چطورن؟
Have a nice day!	ruz khubi dâshte bâshi.	روز خوبی داشته باشی!
Good morning	sobh bekheir	صبح بخیر!
Good evening	asr bekheir	عصر بخیر!
Good night!	shab bekheir	شب بخیر!
Good night!	shab khosh	شب خوش!
Have a good day!	ruz bekheir	روز بخیر!
Have a good time.	oghâte khubi dâshte bâshi.	اوقات خوبی داشته باشی.
Hope to see you again.	omidvâram bâz ham bebinamet.	امیدوارم باز هم ببینمت.
Goodbye.	khodâhâfez.	خداحافظ.
See you later!	Ba'd mibinamet	بعد می بینمت
So long!	be omide didâr	به امید دیدار!

	تشکر کردن	
	Thank You	tashakor kardan
English	**Pronunciation**	**Persian**
Tanks!	mamnun!	ممنون!
Thank you!	mersi	مرسی
Tanks a lot!	kheili mamnunam!	خیلی ممنونم!
Thank you for your help!	mamnun az lotfe shomâ	ممنون از لطف شما!
It was kind of you!	lotf kardi	لطف کردی!
Tank you so much!	kheili azatun mamnunam!	خیلی ازتون ممنونم!
I owe you one.	behet madyunam.	بهت مدیونم.
Thank you for your help!	az komaket mamnunam.	از کمکت ممنونم.
I really appreciate your help!	vâghean az komaket mamnunam.	واقعا از کمکت ممنونم.
I do not know how to thank you!	nemidunam chetor azat tashakor konam!	نمیدونم چطور ازت تشکر کنم!
I really thank you!	vâghean azat mamnunam	واقعاً ازت ممنونم.
It is nice of you.	lotf dâri.	لطف داری.
Thank you for understanding me.	mamnun darkam mikoni.	ممنون درکم می کنی.
Thank you for everything!	vâse hame chiz azat mamnunam.	واسه همه چیز ازت ممنونم!
God bless you!	khodâ kheiret bede!	خدا خیرت بده!
You really helped!	vâghean zahmat keshidi	خیلی زحمت کشیدی!
I didn't want to put you in trouble.	râzi be zahmate shomâ nabudam.	راضی به زحمت شما نبودم.

Answer to Thank you		جواب به تشکر کردن
English	**Pronunciation**	javâb be tashakor kardan **Persian**
You are awesome!	shomâ bozorgvâri.	.شما بزرگواری
You are welcome!	khâhesh mikonam.	.خواهش می کنم
You are welcome!	vazifam bud.	.وظیفم بود
No need to thank.	niyâzi be tashakor nist.	.نیازی به تشکر نیست
You are welcome!	ghorbâne shomâ	!قربان شما
It wasn't a trouble.	zahmati nabud	!زحمتی نبود
No problem!	moshkeli nist!	!مشکلی نیست
Don't mention it!	harfesham nazan	.حرفشم نزن
That's very kind of you!	shomâ lotf dâri	!شما لطف داری
Do not mention it!	ekhtiyâr dâri	!اختیار داری
It wasn't anything special.	Chize khâsi nabud	!چیز خاصی نبود
I didn't do anything.	kâri nakardam	.کاری نکردم
It was nothing.	Chizi nabud	.چیزی نبود
I didn't do anything.	Kâri nabud	.کاری نبود
I did not do anything for you.	kâri barât nakardam.	.کاری برات نکردم
Be healthy!	sâlem bâshi	.سالم باشی
I hope you are healthy.	omidvâram sâlem bâshi.	.امیدوارم سالم باشی
You're kind!	shomâ mehrabuni!	!شما مهربونی

To apologize		معذرت خواهی mazerat khâhi
English	Pronunciation	Persian
I'm sorry!	mazerat mikhâm!	!معذرت میخوام
Sorry!	bebakhshid	.ببخشید
Hope to forgive me.	omidvâram mano bebakhsi.	.امیدوارم منو ببخشی
I didn't mean that.	manzuram in nabud.	.منظورم این نبود
Sorry, I arrived late.	sharmande dir residam.	.شرمنده، دیر رسیدم
I'm really sorry!	vâghean sharmande!	!واقعا شرمنده
Sorry, I don't have time today.	bebakhsh emruz vaght nadâram.	.ببخش امروز وقت ندارم
I'm sorry, I do not have cash.	sharmande, pule naghd nadâram.	.شرمنده، پول نقد ندارم
Sorry, this is my seat.	mazerat mikhâm jâye mane.	!معذرت میخوام جای منه
Sorry, you came home, but I wasn't there.	bebakhshid umadi khune nabudam.	.ببخشید، اومدی خونه نبودم
It's my fault.	taghsire man bud.	.تقصیر من بود
It's my fault.	eshtebâh az man bud	.اشتباه از من بود
I'm sorry, I did not want to interfere.	moteasefam, nemikhâstam dekhâlat konam.	.متاسفم، نمی خواستم دخالت کنم
Sorry, I have a guest.	sharmande mehmun dâram.	.شرمنده مهمون دارم
Sorry! I did not want to upset you!	bebakhsh, namikhâstam nârâhatet konam!	!ببخش نمی خواستم ناراحتت کنم
I'm sorry, I can't tell you.	bebakhsh, namitunam behet begam.	.ببخش، نمیتونم بهت بگم
Sorry. I do not have time now.	sharmande alân vaght nadâram.	.شرمنده الان وقت ندارم
Sorry, I'm in a hurry.	bebakhshid, ajale dâram.	.ببخشید عجله دارم

Answer to apologize	javâb dâdan be mazerat khâhi	جواب دادن به معذرت خواهی
English	Pronunciation	Persian
No problem!	moshkeli nist.	مشکلی نیست.
It's not important.	mohem nist.	مهم نیست.
I forgive you.	mibakhshamet .	می بخشمت.
Do not think about it!	behesh fekr nakon!	بهش فکر نکن!
It dose not matter to me!	vâsam mohem nist!	واسم مهم نیست!
Forget about it.	farâmushesh kon.	فراموشش کن.
Don't mention it.	Khâhesh mikonam	خواهش می کنم.
I just forgot it.	dige farâmush kardam.	دیگه فراموش کردم.
I cannot forgive you!	namitunam bebakhshamet.	نمیتونم ببخشمت.
Do not do it again.	dige tekrâr nashe!	دیگه تکرار نشه!
No need to apologize.	mazerat khâhi lâzem nist.	معذرت خواهی لازم نیست.
It was nothing.	hich etefâghi nayoftâde!	هیچ اتفاقی نیفتاده!
Never mind.	ahamiyati nadâre.	اهمیتی نداره.
It happens.	etefâgh miyofte.	اتفاق می افته.
Do not blam yourself.	khodetu sarzanesh nakon.	خودتو سرزنش نکن.
It dose not matter at all.	aslan mohem nist.	اصلاً مهم نیست.
Do not worry.	negarân nabâsh.	نگران نباش.

Introducing   معرفی کردن

moarefi kardan

English	Pronunciation	Persian
What's your nam?	esmet chiye?	اسمت چیه؟
May name is Reza.	esme man rezâst.	اسم من رضاست.
Who's this boy?	in pesare kiye?	این پسره کیه؟
This is my friend.	in dustame.	این دوستمه.
I'm an Irannian.	Man ahle irân hastam	من اهل ایران هستم.
I'm an American.	Man âmrikâyi hastam	من آمریکایی هستم.
I live in Germany.	Man âlmân zendegi mikonam.	من آلمان زندگی می کنم.
Could you introduce him/her?	mituni oon ro moarefi koni?	میتونی اون رو معرفی کنی؟
Where did you meet each other?	kojâ hamdiga ro didin?	کجا همدیگر رو دیدین؟
Nice to meet uou.	az didant khoshbakhtam.	از دیدنت خوشبختم.
Nice to meet you!	Az didanet khoshhâlam	از دیدنت خوشحالم.
Nice to meet you!	khoshbakhtam	خوشبختم!
Who are you with?	ki hamrâhetune?	کی همراه تونه؟
I am with my family.	man bâ khunevâdam hastam.	من با خونواده ام هستم.
Do you know my friend?	dustam ro mishnâsi?	دوستم رو میشناسی؟
S/he is one of my close friends.	az dustâye samimiye mane.	ازدوستای صمیمی منه.
My friend studies engineering.	dustam mohandesi mikhune.	دوستم مهندسی میخونه.
I came for the holiday.	man vâse tatilât umadam	من واسه تعطیلات اومدم.
I came for business.	man vase kâr umadam.	من واسه کار اومدم.
Do you know me?	mano mishnâsi?	منو می شناسی؟

To Love		دوست داشتن
		dust dâshtan
English	**Pronunciation**	**Persian**
I love you very much!	kheili duset dâram!	خیلی دوستت دارم!
I love you!	man âsheghetam	من عاشقتم!
You are my love!	to eshghe mani	تو عشق منی!
You are my everything.	to hame chize mani.	تو همه چیز منی.
I belong to you.	be tu talogh dâram.	به تو تعلق دارم.
I love you.	behet alâghe dâram.	بهت علاقه دارم.
You are my life.	to zendegiye mani.	تو زندگی منی.
I miss you!	delam barât tang shode!	دلم برات تنگ شده!
I miss you a lot!	delam barât ye zare shode!	دلم برات یه ذره شده!
I always think about you!	hamishe beht fekr mikonam.	همیشه بهت فکر می کنم.
I always think of you.	hamishe be fekretam.	همیشه به فکرتم.
I always think of you.	hamishe be yâdetam	همیشه به یادتم!
Never leave me alone.	hargez man ro tanha nazar.	هرگز من رو تنها نذار.
I'm dying for you!	mimiram barât!	می میرم برات!
I won't forget you.	farâmushet namikonam.	فراموشت نمی کنم.
You are always in my heart.	hamishe tu ghalbami.	همیشه تو قلبمی.
How much do you love him/her?	cheghadr dustesh dâri?	چقدر دوستش داری؟
S/he loves him/her.	Kheili dusesh dâre.	خیلی دوسش داره!
S/he loves you!	un âsheghete!	اون عاشقته!

Like and dislike		دوست داشتن و دوست نداشتن dust dâshtan va dust nadâshtan
English	**Pronunciation**	**Persian**
I like animals.	man heivunâ ro dust dâram.	من حیوونا رو دوست دارم.
I love cooking.	âshpazi ro dust dâram.	آشپزی رو دوست دارم.
I enjoy playing football.	man az bâziye futbâl lezat mibaram.	من از بازی فوتبال لذت میبرم.
I'm crazy about pizza.	man divuneye pitzâ hastam.	من دیوونه پیتزا هستم.
I'm fond of rock music	musighiye râk ro dust dâram.	موسیقی راک رو دوست دارم.
Do you like tennis?	tenis ro dust dâri?	تنیس رو دوست داری؟
I don't like it.	az un khosham nemiyâd.	از اون خوشم نمیاد.
I can't stand these people.	nemitunam in afrâd ro tahamol konam.	نمیتونم این افراد رو تحمل کنم.
I can't stand this smell.	nemitunam in buro tahamol konam.	نمیتونم این بو رو تحمل کنم.
I don't like washing dishes.	shostane zarfâ ro dust nadâram.	شستن ظرفها رو دوست ندارم.
I hate going to the dentist.	man az raftan be dandun pezeshki motenaferam.	من از رفتن به دندون پزشکی متنفرم.
What would you like?	chei dust dâri?	چی دوست داری؟
I enjoyed.	lazat bordam.	لذت بردم.
I really enjoyed!	vâghean lezat bordam.	واقعا لذت بردم.
I like pasta very much.	man kheili pâstâ dust dâram.	من خیلی پاستا دوست دارم.
I don't like to see you.	dust nadâram bebinamet.	دوست ندارم ببینمت.
I don't love you.	dustet nadâram.	دوستت ندارم.

To Agree		موافقت movâfeghat
English	Pronunciation	Persian
Yes!	âre	اره
Yes! That's right!	bale doroste!	بله درسته!
I know.	midunam	می دونم
I understand.	mifahmam.	می فهمم
I completely agree.	kâmelan movâfegham.	کاملاً موافقم.
You're absolutely right.	kâmelan hagh bâ shomâst.	کاملاً حق با شماست.
There is no doubt about it.	Dar moredesh hich shaki nist.	در موردش هیچ شکی نیست.
I agree with you completely.	kâmelan bâhatun movâfegham.	کاملاً باهاتون موافقم.
I agree.	movâfegham.	موافقم.
I see exactly what you mean!	man daghighan midunam manzuretun chiye.	من دقیقاً میدونم منظورتون چیه.
That's exactly what I think.	daghighan hamun chiziye ke fekr mikonam.	دقیقاً همون چیزیه که فکر میکنم.
Me too!	man ham hamintor.	من هم همینطور.
There is no doubt about it	shaki nist.	شکی نیست.
I agree up to a point.	man tâ ye hadi movâfegham.	من تا یه حدی موافقم.
You're right.	hagh bâ shomâst.	حق با شماست.
I agree to some extent.	tâ hododi movâfegham.	تا حدودی موافقم.
Exactly!	daghighan	دقیقا!
Exactly right.	daghighan duroste.	دقیقاً درسته.
You're right!	behetun hagh midam.	بهتون حق میدم.
That's exactly what I meant.	daghighan hamun cheiziye ke manzuram bud.	دقیقاً همون چیزیه که منظورم بود.

To Disagree		mokhâlefat مخالفت
English	Pronunciation	Persian
No!	na	نه
I don't agree!	movafegh nistam.	موافق نیستم.
I don't think so!	fekr nakonam	فکر نکنم.
It's probably not right.	ehtemâlan dorost nist.	احتمالا درست نیست.
I'm sorry, but I disagree.	bebakhshid, vali man mokhâlefam.	ببخشید، ولی من مخالفم.
I'm afraid I can't agree with you.	nemitunam bâhât movâfegh bâsham.	نمیتونم باهات موافق باشم.
It is unacceptable.	gheire ghâbele ghabule.	غیرقابل قبوله.
That's not always true.	hamishe dorost nist.	همیشه درست نیست.
No, that's not true.	na, dorost nist.	نه، درست نیست.
It's wrong!	ghalate	غلطه!
It's wrong!	eshtebâhe	اشتباهه!
I'm not satisfied!	man râzi nistam!	من راضی نیستم!
It is not logical.	in manteghi nist.	این منطقی نیست.
I totally disagree!	kâmelan mokhâlefam.	کاملاً مخالفم.
I don't think so.	fekr namikonam.	فکر نمی کنم.
I cannot accept it.	nemitunam ghabul konam.	نمیتونم قبول کنم.
No way!	be hich vajh.	به هیچ وجه.
It's not acceptable.	aslan ghâbele ghabul nist.	اصلا قابل قبول نیست.
It's not possible!	emkân nadâre!	امکان نداره!

To Ask Questions		سوال پرسیدن soâl porsidan
English	Pronunciation	Persian
Who?	Ki?	کی؟
When?	Kei?	کِی؟
What time?	Che sâati?	چه ساعتی؟
What time?	Che moghe'i?	چه موقعی؟
What time?	Che vaghti?	چه وقتی؟
What day?	Che ruzi?	چه روزی؟
Where?	Kojâ?	کجا؟
Chi?	Chi?	چی؟
Why?	Cherâ?	چرا؟
How much?	Cheghadr?	چقدر؟
For what?	Barâye chi?	برای چی؟
For what reason?	Be che dalili?	به چه دلیلی؟
Who said?	Ki gofte?	کی گفته؟
Where should I go?	Kojâ bâyad beram?	کجا باید برم؟
To whom should I tell?	Be ki begam?	به کی بگم؟
Where are going?	Kojâ dâri miri?	کجا داری می ری؟
With who are you going?	Bâ ki miri?	با کی می ری؟
When will you return?	Kei miyâi?	کِی میای؟
Who is it?	Kiye?	کیه؟
How much is it?	Chande?	چنده؟
What time is it?	Sâat chande?	ساعت چنده؟
What is it?	Chiye?	چیه؟
How?	Chetor?	چطور؟

درک و عدم درک
Understanding and lack of Understanding   dark va adame dark

English	Pronunciation	Persian
Do you understand?	motevaje shodi?	متوجه شدی؟
Do you understand what I mean?	manzuram ro mifahmi?	منظورم رو میفهمی؟
Do you understand what I'm saying?	mifahmi chei migam?	میفهمی چی میگم؟
I don't get it.	man nemidunam.	من نمیدونم.
What do you mean?	manzuret chiye?	منظورت چیه؟
I beg your pardon, but I don't quite understand.	mazerat mikhâm, amâ man kâmelan dark nemikonam.	معذرت می خوام، اما من کاملاً درک نمی کنم.
I don't understand what you mean.	nemidunam manzuretun chiye?	نمیدونم منظورتون چیه؟
Why don't you understand?	cherâ motevaje nemishi?	چرا متوجه نمیشی؟
I don't understand what you said.	nemifahmam chei gofti.	نمی فهمم چی گفتی.
Do you understand what I say?	mifahmi man chei migam?	می فهمی من چی میگم؟
I don't quite follow you.	man kâmelan motevajeye to nemisham.	من کاملاً متوجه تو نمی شم.
I did not get it exactly.	daghighan nafahmidam.	دقیقاً نفهمیدم.
I didn't get it.	man ke nafahmidam.	من که نفهمیدم.
Can you repeat it again?	mituni dobâre tekrâr koni?	میتونی دوباره تکرار کنی؟
Can you say it again?	mishe dobâre begi?	می شه دوباره بگی؟
What did you say?	chi gofti?	چی گفتی؟
What did she/he say?	chi goft?	چی گفت؟
Say it again.	ye bâr dige begu.	یه بار دیگه بگو.
Can you say it again?	mishe ye bâr dige begi?	می شه یه بار دیگه بگی؟

Family	خونواده	
	khunevâde	
English	Pronunciation	Persian
How many brothers and sisters do you have?	chan tâ khâharo barâdar dâri?	چند تا خواهر و برادر داری؟
Where does your father live?	pedare to kojâ zendegi mikone?	پدر تو کجا زندگی می کنه؟
Is she your mother?	un mâdarete?	اون مادرته؟
How many children do you have?	shomâ chand tâ bache dârin?	شما چند تا بچه دارین؟
How many people are in your family?	khunevâdeye shomâ chand nafare hast?	خونواده شما چند نفره هست؟
Do you have a grandfather?	pedarbozorg dâri?	پدربزرگ داری؟
How many uncle (mother's brother) do you have?	chand tâ dâyi dâri?	چند تا دایی داری؟
How many aunt (mother's sister) do you have?	chand tâ khâle dâri?	چند تا خاله داری؟
How many uncle (father's brother) do you have?	chand tâ amu dâri?	چند تا عمو داری؟
How many aunt (father's sister) do you have?	chand tâ ame dâri?	چند تا عمه داری؟
How many brothers and sisters do you have?	barâdare to kojâ zendegi mikone?	برادر تو کجا زندگی می کنه؟
Do you have a younger brother?	barâdare kuchiktar dâri?	برادر کوچیکتر داری؟
Is your sister older than you?	khâharet bozorgtar az toe?	خواهرت بزرگتر از توئه؟
What's your father's job?	bâbât chi kâre hast?	بابات چیکاره هست؟
What's your mother's job?	mâdaret chi kâre hast?	مادرت چیکاره هست؟
What's your brother's job?	shoghle barâdaret chiye?	شغل برادرت چیه؟
What does your sister do?	khâharet chikâre hast?	خواهرت چیکاره هست؟

Clarification and Understanding

توضیح دادن و فهمیدن

tuzih dâdan va fahmidan

English	Pronunciation	Persian
Could you clarify that, please?	lotfan mituni vâzehtar begi?	لطفاً میتونی واضحتر بگی؟
Could you explain that, please?	lotfan mituni tuzih bedi?	لطفاً میتونی توضیح بدی؟
What do you mean by that?	manzuretun chiye?	منظورتون چیه؟
What do you mean?	Manzuret chiye?	منظورت چیه؟
Could you say that again, please?	lotfan mituni dobâre begi?	لطفاً میتونی دوباره بگی؟
Could you repeat, please?	lotfan mituni tekrâr koni?	لطفاً میتونی تکرار کنی؟
Could you put it differently, please?	lotfan mituni motefâvet gharâr bedi?	لطفاً میتونی یه جور دیگه بگی؟
Let me clarify it for you.	ejâze bede in ro shafâf begam.	اجازه بده این رو شفاف بگم.
Let me put it in another way.	Bezâr ye jur dige begam	بزار یه جور دیگه بگم.
I see.	motevajeam.	متوجه ام.
I understand.	mifahmam.	می فهمم.
I got it.	gereftam	گرفتم.
I understand what you mean.	manzutetun ro mifahmam.	منظورتون رو می فهمم.
Can you explain more.	mituni bishtar tuzih bedi.	میتونی بیشتر توضیح بدی.
Let me explain.	bezâr tuzih bedam.	بذار توضیح بدم.
Explain it.	tuzih bede.	توضیح بده.

شکایت کردن
Making a Complaint   shekâyat kardan

English	Pronunciation	Persian
I'm sorry to say this.	moteasefam ke in ro migam.	متاسفم که این رو میگم.
I'm sorry to say this.	bebakhsh ke in ro migam.	ببخش که این رو می گم.
Why are you angry?	cherâ asebâni hasti?	چرا عصبانی هستی؟
There seems to be a problem.	be nazar mirese moshkeli vojud dâre.	به نظر میرسه مشکلی وجود داره.
There is a slight problem with …	ye moshkele joz'i dar morede … vojud dare.	یه مشکل جزئی در مورد .... وجود داره
Sorry to bother you.	bebakhshid ke mozâhem shodam.	ببخشید که مزاحم شدم.
What are you complaining about?	az chei shâki hasti?	از چی شاکی هستی؟
There appears to be something wrong.	be nazaram ye moshkeli hast.	به نظرم یه مشکلی هست.
I want to complain about…	mikhâm dar morede … shekâyat konam	میخوام در مورد ... شکایت کنم.
I have to make a complaint about noise.	man bâyad dar morede saro sedâ shekâyat konam.	من باید در مورد سر و صدا شکایت کنم.
She's always complaining.	un hamishe shâki hast.	اون همیشه شاکی هست.
I don't know why she's complaining.	nemidunam cherâ un shekâyat mikone.	نمیدونم چرا اون شکایت می کنه.
Excuse me but there is a personal problem.	mazerat mikhâm vali in ye moshkele shakhsiye.	معذرت میخوام ولی این یه مشکل شخصیه.
Pleas write your complaint.	lotfan shekâyatet ro benevis.	لطفاً شکایتت رو بنویس.

To Accept or To Refuse a Complaint		قبول یا رد شکایت ghabul va rade shkâyat
English	Pronunciation	Persian
I'm so sorry, but this will never happen again.	kheili moteasefam, vali dige hargez etefâgh nemiyofte.	خیلی متاسفم، ولی دیگه هرگز اتفاق نمی افته.
I'm sorry, I promise not to do it again.	moteasefam, ghol midam dige tekrâr nakonam.	متاسفم قول میدم دیگه تکرار نکنم.
I can't tell you how sorry I am.	nemitunam chetor begam cheghadr moteasefam.	نمیدونم چطور بگم چقدر متاسفم.
It's my fault.	taghsire man bud.	تقصیر من بود.
What can I do to make it right?	che kâri mitunam anjâm bedam tâ un ro durost konam?	چه کاری میتونم انجام بدم تا اون رو درست کنم؟
It was my mistake.	in eshtebâhe man bud.	این اشتباه من بود.
I agree, I made a mistake.	movâfegham, eshtebâh kardam.	موافقم، اشتباه کردم.
You were wrong.	to khodet eshtebâh kardi.	تو خودت اشتباه کردی.
It doesn't matter to me.	vâsam mohem nist.	واسم مهم نیست.
I did not do that.	man in kâr ro nakardam.	من این کار رو نکردم.
I'm innocent.	man bigonâham.	من بی گناهم.
Sorry but it's not my fault.	moteasefam, amâ taghsire man nist.	متاسفم، اما تقصیر من نیست.
I don't blame myself.	khudamo sarzanesh nemikonam.	خودم رو سرزنش نمی کنم.
This is not my problem.	In moshkele man nist.	این مشکل من نیست.
It's none of my business.	Be man rabti nadâre.	به من ربطی نداره.

To Forget and To Remember — فراموشی و یادآوری

farâmoshi va yâd âvari

English	Pronunciation	Persian
Do you know me?	mano mishnâsi?	منو میشناسی؟
I don't remember!	yâdam nemiyâd!	یادم نمیاد!
I do not remember where I met you.	yâdam namiyâd kojâ didamet.	یادم نمیاد کجا دیدمت؟
I did not remember.	yâdam nayumad	یادم نیومد.
Think a little bit.	ye zare fekr kon.	یه ذره فکر کن.
Do you remember where you lost it?	yâdet miyâd kojâ gom kardi?	یادت میاد کجا گم کردی؟
don't forget!	farâmush nakon!	فراموش نکن!
Always remember.	hamishe yâdet bâshe.	همیشه یادت باشه.
I don't remembere anything.	chizi yadam nemiyâd.	چیزی یادم نمیاد.
Have you lost anything?	chizi gom kardi?	چیزی گم کردی؟
I lost something.	man ye chizi gom kardam	من یه چیزی گم کردم.
Do you remember?	yâdet hast?	یادت هست؟
How soon you learned!	che zud yâd gerefti!	چه زود یاد گرفتی!
Remember you promised me!	yâdet bâshe behem ghol dâdi!	یادت باشه بهم قول دادی!
I don't remind you again.	dobâre behet yâdâvari nemikonam.	دوباره بهت یادآوری نمی کنم.
Is this picture familiar to you?	in aks barât âshnâe?	این عکس برات آشنایه؟
Forget about the past.	gozashtaro farâmush kon.	گذشته رو فراموش کن.
I cannot accept it.	nemitunam ghabul konam.	نمی تونم قبول کنم.

Fatigue		خستگی khastegi
English	Pronunciation	Persian
You are tired!	khasteyei	خسته ای!
My job is boring.	kâram khaste konandast.	کارم خسته کنندست.
Take a rest. You get tired.	esterâhat kon khasteh mishi.	استراحت کن، خسته میشی.
I'm tired! I cannot go.	khasteam, namitunam beram.	خسته ام، نمیتونم برم.
We are very tired.	mâ kheili khaste hastim.	ما خیلی خسته هستیم.
I want to sleep.	mikhâm bekhâbam.	میخوام بخوابم.
I'm bored.	hoselam sar rafte.	حوصلم سر رفته.
I feel tired.	ehsâse khastegi mikonam.	احساس خستگی می کنم.
Always sleepy!	hamishe khâb alude!	همیشه خواب آلوده!
I'm so tired.	kheili khastam.	خیلی خسته ام.
You are always tired!	to hamishe khaste hasti	تو همیشه خسته هستی!
Friday is boring.	ruze jome kesel kunandast.	روز جمعه کسل کنندست.
This story is not exciting.	dâstan hayejân nadâreh.	داستان هیجان نداره!
I'm tired of house work.	az kâre khone khastam.	از کار خونه خستم.
He talks a lot, I'm bored!	kheili harf mizane, khstam shod.	خیلی حرف میزنه، خسته شدم.
Aren't you tired?	khaste nisti?	خسته نیستی؟
Take a shower to get rest.	ye dush begir khastegit dar bere.	یه دوش بگیر خستگیت در بره.

To Wait		منتظر بودن
		montazer budan
English	**Pronunciation**	**Persian**
How long does it take?	cheghadr tul mikeshe?	چقدر طول می کشه؟
You have to wait!	bâyad montazer bemuni!	باید منتظر بمونی!
It's oky, I'm waiting for you.	khube, muntazeretam.	خوبه، منتظرتم.
do not wait for me.	muntazere man nabâsh!	منتظر من نباش!
I was waiting for this day.	montazere in ruz budam	منتظر این روز بودم.
How long have you been here?	chand vaghte injâyi?	چند وقته اینجایی؟
Don't hurry.	ajale nakon.	عجله نکن.
I am waiting for you.	montazeretunam.	منتظرتونم.
Wait for a few moments!	chand lahza montazer bâsh!	چند لحظه منتظر باش!
Wait a second!	kami sabr kon!	کمی صبر کن!
How long have you been waiting for me?	cheghadr muntazeram budi?	چقدر منتظرم بودی؟
I'm waiting for you.	cheshm entezâretam.	چشم انتظارتم.
Wait for my call!	montazere tamâsam bâsh!	منتظر تماسم باش!
You know how long have I been waiting?	miduni az key muntazeram?	میدونی از کی منتظرم؟
I was waiting in the waiting room!	dâkhle otâgh entezâr neshastam!	داخل اتاق انتظار منتظر بودم!

Being Happy and Sad		خوشحالی و ناراحتی khoshhâli va nârâhati
English	Pronunciation	Persian
I'm glad to see you.	khosh hâlam didamet.	خوشحالم دیدمت.
I did not want to upset you.	nemikhâstam nârâhatet konam.	نمی خواستم ناراحتت کنم.
Always smile.	hamishe labkhand bezan.	همیشه لبخند بزن.
Do not be so happy!	kheili khoshhâl nabâsh!	خیلی خوشحال نباش!
I'm so sad.	kheili nârâhatam.	خیلی ناراحتم.
Do not worry about me.	negarâne man nabâsh.	نگران من نباش.
What is it? You're happy!	chiye? khoshhâli?	چیه؟ خوشحالی؟
I don't like to see your sadness.	dust nadâram nârâhatit ro bebinam.	دوست ندارم ناراحتیت رو ببینم.
Laugh!	bekhand	بخند!
Always be happy.	hamishe shâd bâsh.	همیشه شاد باش.
I'm so happy!	kheili khoshhâl shodam.	خیلی خوشحال شدم.
Do not upset me!	mano nârâhat nakon!	منو ناراحت نکن!
Everything's perfect!	hamechiz âliye!	همه چیز عالیه!
I'm glad you invited me.	az davatet khoshhâlam.	از دعوتت خوشحالم.
Your life be always full of joy.	zendegit hamishe por âz shâdi.	زندگیت همیشه پر از شادی.
Do not be sad.	nârâhat nabâsh .	ناراحت نباش.

Blaming and Refusing Blaming		سرزنش کردن و رد سرزنش sarzanesh va rade sarzanesh
English	Pronunciation	Persian
It's your fault.	taghsire shomâst.	تقصیر شماست.
It's your mistake.	eshtebâhe shomâst.	اشتباه شماست.
I can't believe that you did it.	bâvaram nemishe shomâ in kâro anjâm dâdi.	باورم نمیشه شما این کار رو انجام دادی.
Are you out of your mind?	aghleto az dast dâdi?	عقلت رو از دست دادی؟
Do not blame me.	mano sarzanesh nakon.	منو سرزنش نکن.
What were you thinking?	chi fekr mikardi.	چی فکر می کردی؟
I think you are the one to blame.	fekr mikonam in shomâ hasti ke bâyad sarzanesh beshi.	فکر می کنم این شما هستی که باید سرزنش بشی
Don't you feel shame?	sharm nemikoni?	شرم نمی کنی؟
Don't you feel shame?	khejâlat nemikeshi?	خجالت نمی کشی؟
It's not true.	in dorost nist.	این درست نیست.
It's not my fault.	man moghaser nistam.	من مقصر نیستم.
I didn't do it.	man in kâro nakardam.	من این کار رو نکردم.
You're wrong. It wasn't me.	eshtebâh kardi. man nabudam.	اشتباه کردی. من نبودم.
I'm not ashamed.	man sharmande nistam.	من شرمنده نیستم.

	تماشای تلویزیون	
Watching TV		tamâshâye televiziyon
English	**Pronunciation**	**Persian**
Turn on the TV.	telviziyon ro roshan kon.	تلویزیون رو روشن کن.
Whte program does it have?	che barnâmeyi dâre?	چه برنامه یی داره؟
Can I change the channel?	mitunam kânâl ro avaz konam?	میتونم کانال روعوض کنم؟
I like this TV show.	man in barnâmaro dust dâram.	من این برنامه رو دوست دارم.
What time dose it begin?	key shorue mishe?	کی شروع میشه؟
Change the channel, I am bored.	kânâl ro avaz kon hoselam sar raft.	کانال رو عوض کن، حوصلم سر رفت.
Whte is your favorite program?	barnâmeye mored alâghat chieye?	برنامه ی مورد علاقه ات چیه؟
I want to watch the movie.	mikhâm film negâh konam.	می خوام فیلم نگاه کنم.
Take a few moments!	chand lahza montazer bâsh!	چند لحظه منتظر باش!
I'm not interesten in TV.	man alâghe'i be telviziyon nadâram.	من علاقه ای به تلویزیون ندارم.
I watched this movie before.	ghablan in film ro didam.	قبلاً این فیلم رو دیدم.
Give me the TV control.	konturole telviziyun ro bede be man	کنترل تلویزیون رو بده به من.
Lower the sound of the tv.	sedâye telviziyon ro kam kon.	صدای تلویزیون رو کم کن.
What movie do you like?	che filmi dust dâri?	چه فیلمی دوست داری؟
I like Persian series.	man seryâle fârsi dust dâram.	من سریال فارسی دوست دارم.
My father likes science fiction.	babâm film elmi takhayoli dust dâre.	بابام فیلم علمی تخیلی دوست داره.

To Help		komak kardan
		کمک کردن
English	Pronunciation	Persian
Let me help you?	bezâr komaket konam?	بذار کمکت کنم؟
I appreciate it if you could help me.	age komakam koni mamnun misham.	اگه کمکم کنی ممنون میشم.
Help me, my car broken!	komakam kon, mâshinam kharâb shode.	کمکم کن، ماشینم خراب شده!
Can you help me?	mishe komakam koni?	میشه کمکم کنی؟
I need your help.	be komaketun niyâz dâram.	به کمکتون نیاز دارم.
Don't worry! I'll help you.	negarân nabâsh. komaket mikonam	نگران نباش. کمکت می کنم.
You helped me a lot.	komake bozorgi behem kardi.	کمک بزرگی بهم کردی.
I helped enouph.	be andâzeye kâfi komak kardam.	به اندازه کافی کمک کردم.
Can I help you?	mitunam komaket konam?	میتونم کمکت کنم؟
Thanks for the donation to the charity.	az komake mâlit be kheiriye mamnunam.	از کمک مالیت به خیریه ممنونم.
Help him/her!	komakesh kon	کمکش کن!
If you can help him/her.	age mituni komakesh kon.	اگه میتونی کمکش کن.
You helped in time.	be moghe komak kardi.	به موقع کمک کردی.
I do not need help.	niyâz be komak nadâram	نیاز به کمک ندارم.
I helped as much as possible!	tâ unjâ ke momken bud komak kardam!	تا اونجا که ممکن بود کمک کردم.

Party		مهمانی
		mehmuni
English	Pronunciation	Persian
When is the party?	mehmuni kei hast?	مهمونی کی هست؟
Who is invited for the party?	Barâye mehmuni ki davate?	برای مهمونی کی دعوته؟
The party is tonight.	Mehmuni emshabe	مهمونی امشبه.
See you tonight!	emshab mibinamet.	امشب می بینمت.
Welcome!	khoshumadi.	خوش اومدی.
It was nice to see you.	az didanet khoshhâlam.	از دیدنت خوشحالم.
Please come in.	lotfan befarmâ tu.	لطفاً بفرما تو.
Long time no see!	kheili vaghte nadidamet!	خیلی وقته ندیدمت!
What do you like to drink?	nushidani chi meil dâri?	نوشیدنی چی میل داری؟
A cup of tea please.	lotfan ye fenjun châi.	لطفا یه فنجون چای.
A cup of coffee please.	lotfan ye fenjun ghahve.	لطفا یه فنجون قهوه.
A glass of water please.	lotfan ye livân âb.	لطفا یه لیوان آب.
Feel free.	râhat bâsh.	راحت باش.
I'm sorry to disturb.	bebakhshid mozâhem shodam.	ببخشید مزاحم شدم.
Did you come by car?	bâ mâshin umadi?	با ماشین اومدی؟
Let me come with you.	ejâze bede hamrât biyâm.	اجازه بده همرات بیام.
Thanks! I'm going	mamnun, dâram miram.	ممنون، دارم میرم.
See you again! Bye!	dobâre mibinamet.	دوباره می بینمت. خداحافظ.

To Invite		دعوت کردن
		davat kardan
English	**Pronunciation**	**Persian**
May I see you today?	mitunam emruz bebinamet?	می تونم امروز ببینمت؟
I would love to see you tomorrow.	dust dâram fardâ bebinamet.	دوست دارم فردا ببینمت.
Can we see each other today?	mitunim emruz hamdigaro bebinim?	می تونیم امروز همدیگرو ببینیم؟
Would you like to come with me?	dust dâri bâ man biyâyi?	دوست داری با من بیایی؟
Would you like to go walking?	dust dâri berim piyâderavi?	دوست داری بریم پیاده روی؟
Com here anytime.	har vaght khâsti biyâ injâ.	هر وقت خواستی بیا اینجا.
How many people do you want to invite?	chand nafar mikhâi davat koni	چند نفر میخوای دعوت کنی؟
I'll treat you.	mehmun man bâsh.	مهمون من باش.
Thank you for accepting my invitation.	mamnun davatam ro ghabul kardi.	ممنون دعوتم رو قبول کردی.
Tonight we are invited for dinner.	emshab shâm davatim.	امشب شام دعوتیم.
What's your plan for tonight?	barnâmatun vâse emshab chiye?	برنامه تون واسه امشب چیه؟
Would you like to go shopping?	dust dâri berim kharid?	دوست داری بریم خرید؟
Do you have free time tomorrow?	fardâ vaght dâri?	فردا وقت داری؟
I want to see you.	mikhâm bebinamet.	میخوام ببینمت.
I'll send an invitation card.	man ye karte davat mifrestam	من یه کارت دعوت می فرستم.
I invited him/her for dinner tonight.	emshab uno barâye shâm davit kardam.	امشب اون رو برای شما دعوت کردم.

پذیرفتن دعوت
Accepting Invitation — paziroftane davat

English	Pronunciation	Persian
Thank you for your invitation.	az davatet mamnunam.	از دعوتت ممنونم.
Many thanks for your invitation.	kheili mamnun vâse davatetun	خیلی ممنون واسه دعوتتون.
I'd love to, thanks.	man dust dâram ,mamnun.	من دوست دارم، ممنون.
I'll be glad to do so.	khoshhâl misham in kâr ro anjâm bedam.	خوشحال میشم این کار رو انجام بدم.
Thanks, I'd like that very much.	mamnun, kheili dust dâram.	ممنون خیلی دوست دارم.
Sure. Thank you.	khâter jam. mamnunam.	خاطر جمع، ممنونم.
That's a great idea.	fekre khubiye.	فکر خوبیه.
Thank you for inviting me for dinner.	mamnun man ro shâm davat kardi.	ممنون من رو شام دعوت کردی.
With pleasure!	bâ kamâle meil.	با کمال میل.
It's very nice of you.	nazare lotfetune.	نظر لطفتونه.
What's better than this.	che behtar az in.	چه بهتر از این.
I will definitely come.	motmaenan miyâm.	مطمئناً میام.
I accept your invitation.	davatet ro ghabul mikonam.	دعوتت رو قبول می کنم.
Could not be better.	behtar az in nemitunest beshe.	بهتر از این نمیتونست بشه.
I'm honored to be with you.	eftekhâr mikonam bâhâtun bâsham.	افتخار می کنم باهاتون باشم.

Refusing Invitation		نپذیرفتن دعوت napaziruftane davat
English	**Pronunciation**	**Persian**
I'm sorry to refuse your invitation.	moteasefam ke davatet ro rad mikonam.	متاسفم که دعوتت رو رد می کنم.
I can't, sorry. I have to work.	nemitunam, mazerat mikhâm. bâyad kâr konam.	نمیتونم، معذرت میخوام، باید کار کنم.
Thanks for your invitation but I'm busy now.	mamnun az davatet vali alân gereftâram.	ممنون از دعوتت ولی الان گرفتارم.
I'm afraid, I won't be able to come.	bebakhshid, nemitunam biyâm.	ببخشید، نمیتونم بیام.
Sorry, I am busy tomorrow.	sharmande, farâd mashghulam.	شرمنده، فردا مشغولم.
Sorry, I'd love to but I have an appointment.	sharmande, dust dâram vali gharâre molâghât dâram.	شرمنده، دوست دارم ولی قرار ملاقات دارم.
I really don't think I can, sorry.	vâghean fekr nemikonam betunam, sharmande.	واقعاً فکر نمیکنم بتونم، شرمنده.
That's very kind of you, but I can't accept your invitation.	vâghean lotf dâri, vali nemitunam davatet ro ghabul konam.	واقعاً لطف داری، ولی نمیتونم دعوتت رو قبول کنم.
I will not promise.	ghol nemidam.	قول نمیدم.
Sorry, I have some works to do.	sharmande, chand tâ kâr dâram.	شرمنده چند تا کار دارم.

Certainty		مطمئن شدن
		motmaen shodan
English	Pronunciation	Persian
Are you sure?	motmaeni?	مطمئنی؟
Are you sure about it?	dar morede un motmaeni?	در مورد اون مطمئنی؟
Yes, I am sure.	âre, man motmaenam.	آره، من مطمئنم.
I'm a hundred percent sure.	sad dar sad motmaenam.	صد در صد مطمئنم.
I'm absolutely sure.	kâmelan motmaenam.	کاملاً مطمئنم.
I have no doubt about it.	dar morede un shak nadâram.	در مورد اون شک ندارم.
I'm sure about it.	dar morede un motmaenam.	در مورد اون مطمئنم.
I don't think there can be any doubt about ….	man fekr nemikonam shak va tardidi vojud dâshte bâshe.	من فکر نکنم شک و تردیدی وجود داشته باشه.
Of course.	albate.	البته.
I'm quite sure about it.	man kâmelan dar morede un motmaenam.	من کاملاً در مورد اون مطمئنم.
I have no doubt.	man shak nadâram.	من شک ندارم.
Don't be skeptical.	shak nakon.	شک نکن.
Be sure.	motmaen bâsh.	مطمئن باش.
How are you sure?	chetor motmaeni?	چطور مطمئنی؟

Uncertainty	مطمئن نبودن	
English	Pronunciation	Persian
I'm not sure about it.	dar morede un motmaen nistam.	در مورد اون مطمئن نیستم.
I doubt it.	shak dâram.	شک دارم.
I'm not really sure.	vâghean motmaen nistam.	واقعاً مطمئن نیستم.
I don't know for sure.	motmaenam nistam.	مطمئن نیستم.
It's very unlikely.	kheili baide.	خیلی بعیده.
I have my own doubts.	man tardid dâram.	من تردید دارم.
I don't think so.	gamun nemikonam..	گمون نمی کنم.
I don't believe this is true.	bâvar nadâram in durost bâshe.	باور ندارم این درسته باشه.
Maybe it's true.	shâyad dorost bâshe.	شاید درست باشه.
I'm not a hundred percent sure.	sad dar sad motmaen nistam.	صد در صد مطمئن نیستم.
I don't know yet.	hanuz nemidunam.	هنوز نمیدونم.
I don't know precisely.	daghighan nemidunam.	دقیقاً نمیدونم.

motmaen nabudan.

درخواست کردن
To Request — darkhâst kardan

English	Pronunciation	Persian
Excuse me, can you help me?	bebakhshid mituni behem komak koni?	ببخشید، می تونی بهم کمک کنی؟
Please repeat that one more time.	lotfan ye bâr dige tekrâr kon.	لطفاً یه بار دیگه تکرار کن.
I'm asking you.	dâram azat darkhâst mikonam.	دارم ازت درخواست می کنم.
Please hurry up!	lotfan ajale kon!	لطفاً عجله کن!
Can you call a taxi?	momkene ye tâksi sedâ koni?	ممکنه یه تاکسی صدا کنی؟
Can I have your address?	mitunam âdreset ro begiram?	می تونم آدرست رو بگیرم؟
Can you take me to the airport?	mituni mano bebari forudgâh?	می تونی منو ببری فرودگاه؟
Can you be silent?	mituni sâket bâshi?	میتونی ساکت باشی؟
Could I take a look at it?	mitunam negâsh konam?	میتونم نگاش کنم ؟
Can you post this letter?	mituni in nâme ro post koni?	میتونی این نامه رو پست کنی؟
Please speak more slowly	lotfan âhestetar sohbat kon.	لطفاً آهسته تر صحبت کن.
May I borrow your journal?	mitunam majalatun ro gharz begiram?	می تونم مجله تون رو قرض بگیرم؟
I can ask you a question?	mitunam azat ye soâl beporsam?	میتونم ازت یه سوال بپرسم؟
Can you hold this?	mituni in ro negah dâri?	میتونی این رو نگه داری؟
Can I borrow money?	mituni pul behem gharz bedi?	میتونی پول بهم قرض بدی؟
Please fill the employment form.	lotfan forme estekhdâmo por kon.	لطفاً فرم استخدامو پر کن.
I want you to forgive me this time!	azat mikhâm inbâr mano bebakhshi!	ازت میخوام این بار منو ببخشی!

Feelings and Blessing — احساسات و دعای خیر

ehsâsât va doâye kheir

English	Pronunciation	Persian
Everything will be fine.	hamechi dorost mishe.	همه چیز درست می شه.
I am so excited!	kheili hayejân zadeam!	خیلی هیجان زده م!
I feel bad.	hâlam kheili bade.	حالم خیلی بده.
Congratulations!	tabrik migam!	تبریک میگم!
Happy new year!	sâle no mobârak	سال نو مبارک!
Good luck.	movafagh bâshi.	موفق باشی.
Have a nice trip!	safare khubi dâshte bâshi!	سفر خوبی داشته باشی!
Have a good time!	ôghâte khubi dâshte bâshin!	اوقات خوبی داشته باشین!
Enjoy!	khosh begzare!	خوش بگذره!
Happy new year!	sad sâl be in sâlhâ!	صد سال به این سالها!
I hope you always be successful.	omidvâram hamishe movafagh bâshi.	امیدوارم همیشه موفق باشی.
You deserve the best.	to lâyeghe behtarinhâyi.	تو لایق بهترین هایی.
I hope you are healthy!	umidvâram sâlm bâshi!	امیدوارم سالم باشی!
Always be happy in your life.	hamhamishe tu zendegit shâd bâshi.	همیشه تو زندگیت شاد باشی.
I'm so eager to see him/her!	kheili moshtâgham bebinamesh!	خیلی مشتاقم ببینمش!

To be Shocked	shoke shodan	شوکه شدن
English	Pronunciation	Persian
We're all in complete shock.	mâ kâmelan shoke shodim.	ما کاملاً شوکه شدیم.
I was surprised!	kheili ta'ajob kardam.	خیلی تعجب کردم!
Who could have predicted it?	key mitunest un ro pishbini kone?	کی میتونست اون رو پیش بینی کنه؟
Are you kidding!	dâri shukhi mikoni!	داری شوخی می کنی!
It was unexpected.	gheire montazere bud.	غیرمنتظره بود.
I never thought of that.	hargez fekresh nemikardam.	هرگز فکرش نمی کردم.
I could guess.	mitunestam hads bezanam.	می تونستم حدس بزنم.
Oh, my god! Really?	vây, khodâye man! vâghean.	وای، خدای من! واقعاً!
No one believed.	hich kas bâvar nadâsht.	هیچ کس باور نداشت.
I was shocked to hear.	shoke shodam shenidam.	شوکه شدم شنیدم.
It was shocking.	shoke ajibi bud.	شوک عجیبی بود.
I'm shocked, I don't know what to say.	shoke shodam, nemidunam chi begam.	شوکه شدم، نمیدونم چی بگم.
I did not expect.	entezâr nadâshtam.	انتظار نداشتم.
I don't know how to give this news!	nemidunam chetor in khabar ro bedam!	نمیدونم چطور این خبر رو بدم.
I can't believe this!	nemitunam ino bâvar konam.	نمی تونم این رو باور کنم!

	تعریف کردن	
	To Praise ta'rif kardan	
English	**Pronunciation**	**Persian**
Your hair style is very good.	modele muhât kheili khube!	!مدل موهات خیلی خوبه
Your selection is great!	entekhâbet âliye	!انتخابت عالیه
Your effort is very good!	talâshet kheili khube	!تلاشت خیلی خوبه
That's very kind of you!	vâghean lotf dâri!	!واقعاً لطف داری
It is very good!	kheili khube!	!خیلی خوبه
You look happy!	khoshhâl be nazar miresi	!خوشحال به نظر می رسی
I'm always proud of you.	man hamishe behet eftekhâr mikonam.	!من همیشه بهت افتخار میکنم
Your food is delicious!	ghazâtun khoshmaze hast!	!غذاتون خوشمزه هست
S/he has a good talent.	estedâde khubi dâre.	.استعداد خوبی داره
Wow, What a romantic one!	vây!che romântik!	!وای! چه رمانتیک
What a beautiful place!	cheghadr jâye ghashangiye!	!چقدر جای قشنگیه
What a beautiful name you have!	che esme ghashangi dâri	!چه اسم قشنگی داری
What a nice view!	che manzareye khubi!	!چه منظره خوبی
S/he has a very good mood.	akhlâghesh kheili khube.	.اخلاقش خیلی خوبه
You look great!	âli be nazar miyâi!	!عالی به نظر میای

آب و هوا
The Weather — âbo havâ.

English	Pronunciation	Persian
Today is sunny.	emruz havâ âftâbiye!	!امروز هوا آفتابیه
Today is warm.	emruz havâ garme.	.امروز هوا گرمه
Today is cold.	emruz havâ sarde.	.امروز هوا سرده
It's cold and freezing!	sardo yakhbandune!	!خیلی سرد و یخبندونه
Thunderstorm.	tufân - ra'do bargh.	.توفان - رعد و برق
How is the weather there?	havâ unjâ chetore?	هوای اونجا چطوره؟
It's dusty here.	injâ gardo khâke.	.اینجا گرد و خاکه
The weather is polluted today.	emruz havâ âludast.	.امروز هوا آلودست
It's claudy.	havâ abriye	.هوا ابریه
Here it's raining.	injâ bârun miyâd.	.اینجا بارون میاد
The southern is hot and dry!	havâye jonub garmo khoshke!	!هوای جنوب گرم و خشکه
It's snowing.	dâre barf miyâd	.داره برف میاد
What a beautiful rainbow!	che ranginkamâne ghashangi!	!چه رنگین کمان قشنگی
Today the weather is good.	emruz havâye khubiye	!امروز هوای خوبیه
It was cold in the morning.	havâ sobh sard bud.	.هوا صبح سرد بود
How is the weather today?	emruz havâ chetore?	امروز هوا چطوره؟
Tomorrow is very cold.	fardâ havâ kheili sarde	.فردا هوا خیلی سرده

Time & Date

زمان و تاریخ

zamân va târikh

English	Pronunciation	Persian
What time is it?	sâat chande?	ساعت چنده؟
Time flies.	zamân zud gozasht.	زمان زود گذشت.
Do you know what time it is?	miduni sâat chnde?	میدونی ساعت چنده؟
How long have you been waiting?	cheghadr montazer budi?.	چقدر منتظر بودی؟
Do you have free time this afternoon?	emruz asr vaghte âzâd dâri?	امروز عصر وقت آزاد داری؟
When can we meet?	key mitunim hamdige ro bebinim?	کی میتونیم همدیگه رو ببینیم؟
The class starts at 8.	kelâs sâat hasht shoru mishe.	کلاس ساعت هشت شروع میشه.
It's mid night.	nesfe shabe.	نصف شبه.
It's too late now.	alân kheili dir shode	الان خیلی دیر شده.
My watch is slow.	sâatm aghab oftâde.	ساعتم عقب افتاده.
I didn't think it was so late.	fekr nemikardam kheili dir bâshe.	فکر نمی کردم خیلی دیر باشه.
We have plenty of time.	mâ kheili vaght dârim.	ما خیلی وقت داریم.
Give me a little more time.	ye kam bishtar behem vaght bede.	یه کم بیشتر بهم وقت بده.
It's time to go.	vaghte raftane.	وقت رفتنه.
My watch is stopped.	sâatm khâbide.	ساعتم خوابیده.
I'll come in two hours.	do sâat dige miyâm	دو ساعت دیگه میام.
What time will you come?	sâat chand miyâi?	ساعت چند میای؟
When will we go?	kei mirim?	کی میریم؟

		اخطار
Warning		ekhtâr
English	Pronunciation	Persian
Be careful!	movâzeb bash!	مواظب باش!
Pay more attention!	bishtar deghat kon!	بیشتر دقت کن!
Be very cautious!	kheili ehtiyât kon!	خیلی احتیاط کن!
Take care!	movâzebe khodet bâsh!	مواظب خودت باش!
Be ready!	amâde bâsh!	آماده باش!
I warned you!	behet hoshdâr dâdam!	بهت هشدار دادم!
Never hurry!	hargez ajale nakon	هرگز عجله نکن!
There is a danger of drowning!	khtare ghargh shodan hast	خطر غرق شدن هست.
I remainded her!	behesh yâdâvari kardam!	بهش یادآوری کردم!
Do not repeat it again!	dobâre tekrâr nakon!	دوباره تکرار نکن!
Get serious about safety!	imeni ro jedi begir!	ایمنی رو جدی بگیر!
Entry is forbidden!	vorud mamnue!	ورود ممنوعه!
How many times should I tell you?	chand bâr behet begam?	چند بار بهت بگم؟
I repeated it several times!	man chand bâr tekrâr kardam!	من چند بار تکرار کردم!
I said it seriously.	kâmelan jedi goftam	کاملاً جدی گفتم.

بیان عقاید

Expression of Opinions — bayân aghâied

English	Pronunciation	Persian
I think It's a good idea.	fekr mikonam fekre khubiye.	فکر می کنم فکر خوبیه.
I feel that she is tired.	hes mikonam khaste shode.	حس می کنم خسته شده.
What do you think of me?	dar mored man chie fekr mikoni?	در مورد من چی فکر می کنی؟
I don't think it's rational.	fekr nemikonam manteghi bâshe.	فکر نمیکنم منطقی باشه.
your opinion is more important.	nazare khodet mohemtare.	نظر خودت مهمتره.
I have no idea.	hich nazari nadâram.	هیچ نظری ندارم.
I have not doubt that he will win.	man shak nadâram un barande mishe.	من شک ندارم اون برنده میشه.
Your opinion is respectful to me	nazaret vâsam mohtarâme.	نظرت واسم محترمه.
I think it's better to tell him.	fekr konam behtare behesh begam.	فکر کنم بهتره بهش بگم.
My opinion was not important.	nazaram mohem nabud!	نظرم مهم نبود!
I think it's better to consult.	be nazaram behtare mashverat koni.	به نظرم بهتره مشورت کنی.
It's better to say your opinion.	behtare nazareto begi.	بهتره نظرتو بگی.
I think she's lying.	fekr mikonam durugh mighe?	فکر میکنم دروغ میگه.
I do not think so.	man intur fekr nemikonam.	من اینطور فکر نمی کنم.
My opinion will not change.	raye man avaz nemishe.	رای من عوض نمیشه.

ازدواج
Marriage   ezdevâj

English	Pronunciation	Persian
I'm single.	man mojaradam	من مجردم.
I'm married.	man moteahelam	من متاهلم.
I'm married.	man zan dâram	من زن دارم!
Are you married?	to ezdevâj kardi?	تو ازدواج کردی؟
I want to marry her.	mikhâm bâ un ezdevâj konam.	میخوام با اون ازدواج کنم.
I congratulate you.	behet tabrik migam.	بهت تبریک میگم.
I am engaged.	man nâmzad dâram.	من نامزد دارم.
I want go to honeymoon.	mikhâm beram mâhe asal.	میخوام برم ماه عسل.
He proposed to her.	un behesh pishnahâd dâd.	اون بهش پیشنهاد داد.
Happy anniversary!	sâlgarde ezdevâjetun mobârak.	سالگرد ازدواجتون مبارک.
I hope you always be happy.	umidvâram hamishe shâd bâshi.	امیدوارم همیشه شاد باشی.
Where do you have a wedding?	arusi kojâs?	عروسی کجاست؟
How long have you been married?	chand vaghte ezdevâj kardi?	چند وقته ازدواج کردی؟
Which city is your wife come from?	az kodum shahr zan gerefti?	از کدوم شهر زن گرفتی؟
I love marrying you.	dust dâram bâhat ezdevâj konam.	دوست دارم باهات ازدواج کنم.
Come for our wedding.	arusiye mâ biyâ.	عروسی ما بیا.
I do not think of marriage.	be ezdevâj fekr namikonam.	به ازدواج فکر نمی کنم.
I don't want to marry now.	felan namikhâm ezdevâj konam.	فعلاً نمی خوام ازدواج کنم.
I wish you happiness!	barâtun ârezuye khoshbakhti dâram!	براتون آرزوی خوشبختی دارم!

	آپارتمان/ خونه	
	Apartment / House	âpârtemân / khune
English	**Pronunciation**	**Persian**
Where do you live?	kojâ zendgi mikoni?	کجا زندگی می کنی؟
I am in a residential complex.	man tu ye mojtamae maskuniyam.	من تو یه مجتمع مسکونیم.
I live first floor.	tabegheye aval zendegi mikonam.	طبقه اول زندگی می کنم.
I want to sell the apartement.	mikhâm âpartemân ro befrusham.	میخوام آپارتمان رو بفروشم.
90 meters, two bedroom	navad metr, do khâbe	۹۰ متر دو خوابه.
Do you have parking?	Pârking dârin?	پارکینگ دارین؟
Where is your home?	Khuneye to kojâst?	خونه تو کجاست؟
How much is the apartment to buy?	gheimate âpârtemân chande?	قیمت آپارتمان چنده؟
I go to real estate.	miram bongâhe amlâk.	میرم بنگاه املاک.
Where did you buy your apartment?	âpârtemânet ro kojâ kharidi?	آپارتمانت رو کجا خریدی؟
Does have a play ground for kids?	muhavateye bâzi vâse bachehâ dâre?	محوطه بازی واسه بچه ها داره؟
Is your apartment big?	âpârtemânet bozorge?	آپارتمانت بزرگه؟
Do you pay monthly fees?	hazineye mâhâne pardâkht mikoni?	هزینه ماهانه پرداخت می کنی؟
I want to see the property manager.	mikhâm modire sâkhtemun ro bebinam.	میخوام مدیر ساختمون رو ببینم.
The elevator has been broken for a few days.	âsânsor chand ruze kharâb shode.	آسانسور چند روزه خراب شده.
Somebody needs to clean our building.	ye nafar vâseye nezâfate sâkhtemun lâzeme.	یه نفر واسه نظافت ساختمون لازمه.
I want to lease an apartment	mikhâm ye âpartemân ejâre konam.	میخوام یه آپارتمان اجاره کنم.

Feelings	ehsâsât	احساسات
English	Pronunciation	Persian
I'm so sad.	Kheili nârâhatam	خیلی ناراحتم.
Sorry!	moteasefam	متاسفم.
I'm so sorry!	kheili moteasefam !	خیلی متاسفم!
I feel bad.	Hâlam bade	حالم بده.
Today I feel good!	Emruz hâlam kheili khube.	امروز حالم خیلی خوبه!
I'm very happy right now.	alân kheili khoshhâlam.	الان خیلی خوشحالم.
I don't feel well.	ehsâse khubi nadarâm.	احساس خوبی ندارم.
I feel a little sad.	man kami nârâhatam	من کمی ناراحتم.
I'm bored!	Hoselam sar rafte.	حوصله ام سر رفته!
I hate him/her.	azash motenaferam.	ازش متنفرم.
Control your feelings.	ehsâsâte khodeto kontorol kon.	احساسات خودتو کنترل کن.
Do not worry about me.	negarâne man nabâsh.	نگران من نباش.
I'm very happy.	kheili khoshhâl shodam.	خیلی خوشحال شدم.
Do not blame yourself at all.	aslan khodeto sarzanesh nakon.	اصلاً خودتو سرزنش نکن.
I feel good with you.	bâ to ehsâse khubi dâram.	با تو احساس خوبی دارم.
I feel pity for him.	man barâsh moteasefam.	من براش متاسفم.
What a pity I did not meet you!	che heif shod nadidamet!	چه حیف شد ندیدمت!
Do not upset me.	mano nârâhat nakon.	منو ناراحت نکن.
I was excited!	hayejân zade shodam!	هیجان زده شدم!

Making Offers — پیشنهاد دادن

pishnahâd dadan.

English	Pronunciation	Persian
Would you like something to eat?	dust dâri chizi bokhori?	دوست داری چیزی بخوری؟
Would you like me to open the door?	mikhây man daro bâz konam?	میخوای من در رو باز کنم؟
Can you help me?	mituni komakam koni?	میتونی کمکم کنی؟
Can I give you a hand?	mitunam komaket konam?	میتونم کمکت کنم؟
Let me help you.	ejâze bede behet komak konam?	اجازه بده بهت کمک کنم.
Would you like to answer the phone?	mikhây be telefun javâb bedi?	میخوای به تلفن جواب بدی؟
Do you want me to turn down the TV?	mikhây telviziyon ro khâmush konam?	میخوای تلویزیون رو خاموش کنم؟
I'd happy to take you to the airport.	khoshhâl misham shomâ ro bebaram forudgâh	خوشحال می شم شما رو ببرم فرودگاه.
May I offer you a cup of coffee.	ye fenjun ghahve mikhorin?	یه فنجون قهوه می خورین؟
Would you like me to go out?	mikhây beram birun?	میخوای برم بیرون؟
Let me come with you.	ejâze bede bâhât biyâm	اجازه بده باهات بیام.
Would you like to travel?	mikhây beri safar?	میخوای بری مسافرت؟
Go with my car.	bâ mâshine man boro.	با ماشین من برو.
Do you need anything?	chizi lâzem dâri?	چیزی لازم داری؟
Don't you need anything?	chizi nemikhây?	چیزی نمی خوای؟

	درخواست دادن	
	Making requests darkhast dâdan	

English	Pronunciation	Persian
Could you please open the door?	mituni dar ro bâz koni?	می تونی در رو باز کنی؟
Could you please close the windows?	mituni parjara ro bebandi?	می تونی پنجره رو ببندی؟
Can you bring me a glass of water?	mituni barâm ye livân âb biyâri?	می تونی برام یه لیوان آب بیاری؟
Can you give me a cup of tea?	mituni ye livân chây be man bedi?	می تونی یه لیوان چای به من بدی؟
Can you give me the book?	mituni ketâb ro be man bedi?	میتونی کتاب رو به من بدی؟
Could you please take me to the dentist?	lotfan mituni man ro bebari dandun pezeshki?	لطفاً میتونی من رو ببری دندون پزشکی؟
Would you mind opening the window for me, please?	lotfan panjere ro vâsam bâz mikoni?	لطفاً پنجره رو واسم باز می کنی؟
Could you please repair my computer?	mituni kâmpiyuteram ro dorost koni?	می تونی کامپیوترم رو درست کنی؟
Could I ask you to take me home?	mitunam azat bekhâm mano be khune bebari?	میتونم ازت بخوام من رو به خونه ببری؟
Can you tell me what happened?	mituni be man begi chi shode?	میتونی به من بگی چه شده؟
Would you come to my birthday party?	jashne tavalode man miyây?	جشن تولد من میای؟
Would it be possible for you to come at 8?	momkene sâate hasht biyây?	ممکنه ساعت هشت بیای؟
Can I call you now?	alân mitunam behet zang bezanam?	الان میتونم بهت زنگ بزنم؟
Do you have time to meet?	vaght dâri hamdiga ro bebinim?	وقت داری همدیگر رو ببینیم؟

Refusing Requests and Accepting Requests

رد و قبول کردن درخواستها — rad ve ghbol kardan darkhâsthâ

English	Pronunciation	Persian
OK!	bâshe	باشه.
For sure!	hatman	حتما.
No problem.	moshkeli nist.	مشکلی نیست.
Of course	albate.	البته.
Sure, I'd be glad to.	albate, khoshhâl misham.	البته، خوشحال میشم.
I'd be happy to help.	khoshhâl misham komak konam.	خوشحال می شم کمک کنم.
Certainly.	ghat an.	قطعاً.
Alright.	kheili khob.	خیلی خوب.
Sure. Just a moment.	hatman, ye lahze.	حتما، یه لحظه.
I will Certainly come.	man ghat an miyâm.	من قطعاً میام.
It's good. But I cannot come with you.	khube, amâ man nemitunam bâhâtun biyâm.	خوبه، اما من نمیتونم باهاتون بیام.
I'm sorry, I can't.	moteasefam. man nemitunam.	متاسفم من نمیتونم.
I'm not sure I can come.	motmaen nistam betunam biyâm.	مطمئن نیستم بتونم بیام.
It look great, but I don't like it.	be nazar âleiye, amâ dust nqadâram.	به نظر عالیه، ولی دوست ندارم.
Sorry. I cannot go today.	sharmande. emruz nemitunam beram.	شرمنده ، امروز نمیتونم برم.
I cannot do it.	nemitunam anjâmesh bedam.	نمیتونم انجامش بدم.

Accepting Offers and Refusing Offers

رد و قبول پیشنهادات

rad va ghabool pishnahâdât

English	Pronunciation	Persian
Yes, please.	bale, lotfan.	بله لطفاً
Yes, I'd love to.	âre, dust daram	آره، دوست دارم.
Yes. That would be great.	bale, âli mishe.	بله، عالی میشه.
Yes please, that would be great.	bale lotfan, kheili khub mishe.	بله لطفاً، خیلی خوب می شه.
That sounds nice.	jâleb be nazar mirese.	جالب به نظر میرسه.
Thank you. I'd like to.	mamnun, dust daram.	ممنون، دوست دارم
Your proposal is awesome.	pishnahâdet âliye.	پیشنهادت عالیه.
No, thanks.	na. mamnun.	نه، ممنون
Not a bad idea.	fekere badi nist.	فکر بدی نیست.
It's Ok. I can do it myself.	khube, mitunam khodam anjâm bedam.	خوبه، میتونم خودم انجام بدم.
Thank you for your kindness but I can do it myself.	az lotfetun mamnunam, amâ khodam mitunam anjâm bedam.	ازلطفتون ممنونم، اما خودم میتونم انجام بدم.
Don't worry. I can do it.	negarân nabâsh, mitunam anjâm bedam.	نگران نباش، میتونم انجام بدم.
I appreciate that but I can do it myself.	mamnunam, vali khodam mitunam anjâm bedam.	ممنونم، ولی خودم میتونم انجام بدم.
I cannot accept you'r offer.	nemitunam pishnahâdet ro ghabul konam.	نمیتونم پیشنهادت رو قبول کنم.

	شغل	
	Job shoghl	
English	Pronunciation	Persian
What is your occupation?	shoghlet chiye?	شغلت چیه؟
I'm not working at the moment.	alân kâr nemikonam.	الان کار نمی کنم.
I'm unemployed.	bikâram.	بیکارم.
Where do you work?	kojâ kâr mikoni?	کجا کار می کنی؟
I work for a company.	vâse ye sherkat kâr mikonam.	واسه یه شرکت کار می کنم.
Are you satisfied with your job?	az shoghlet râzi hasti?	از شغلت راضی هستی؟
How much is your income?	darâmadetun cheghadre?	درآمدتون چقدره؟
I want to leave my job!	mikhâm kâram ro vel konam!	میخوام کارم رو ول کنم!
I did not find my favorit job.	kare morede alâgham ro peidâ nakardam.	کار موردعلاقه م رو پیدا نکردم.
Frist safety then work!	aval imeni bad kâr!	اول ایمنی بعد کار!
Have you been insured?	bime shodi?	بیمه شدی؟
Do you have part time work?	kâre nime vaght dâri?	کار نیمه وقت داری؟
I'm not satisfied with my job.	az kâram râzi nistam.	از کارم راضی نیستم.
I lost my job!	shoghlam ro az dast dâdam!	شغلم رو ازدست دادم!
Do you have a healthcare directory?	daftarche khadamâte darmâni dâri?	دفترچه خدمات درمانی داری؟
Do you have enouph experience in this job?	vâse in kâr tajrobeye kâfi dâri?	واسه این کار تجربه کافی داری؟
Do you like your business?	kâret ro dust dâri?	کارت رو دوست داری؟
Do you have any work history.	sâbegheye kâr dâri?	سابقه کار داری؟

	آینده	
	Future âyande	
English	Pronunciation	Persian
What are you plan for the future?	barnâmat vâse âyande chiye?	برنامه ات واسه آینده چیه؟
Hop you have a good future	omidvâram âyandeye khubi dâshte bâshi.	امیدوارم آینده خوبی داشته باشی.
I hope for the future.	be âyande omidvâram.	به آینده امیدوارم.
It has a brilliant future.	âyandeye derakhshâni dâre.	آینده درخشانی داره.
The future can not be foreseen.	âyande ro namishe pishbini kard.	آینده رو نمیشه پیش بینی کرد.
We have to build the future.	âyanda ro bâyad besâzim.	آینده رو باید بسازیم.
Hope you succeed in the future.	omidvâram dar âyande movafagh bâshi.	امیدوارم در آینده موفق باشی.
You must be futuristic.	bâyad âyande negar bâshi.	باید آینده نگر باشی.
do not worry about the future of the kids.	darbâre âyande bachahâ negarân nabâsh.	درباره آینده بچه ها نگران نباش.
What's you plan for the weekend?	barnâmat barâye âkhare hafte chiye?	برنامت برای آخر هفته چیه؟
What are you going to do tomorrow?	fardâ mikhây chikâr koni?	فردا می خوای چیکار کنی؟
Good days are coming.	ruz hâye khubi miyâd.	روزهای خوبی میاد.
I want to be an engineer in the future.	dar âyande mikhâm mohandes besham.	درآینده میخوام مهندس بشم.
Have a good future.	âyande khubi dâshte bâshi.	آینده خوبی داشته باشی.
Always look forward to yourfuture.	hamishe negâhet be âyande bâshe.	همیشه نگاهت به آینده باشه.

News		خبرها
	khabarhâ	
English	Pronunciation	Persian
Hope you have good news.	omidvâram khabare khubi dâshte bâshi.	امیدوارم خبر خوبی داشته باشی.
What's the price of a newspaper	gheimate ruznâme chande?	قیمت روزنامه چند؟
Did you hear the news today?	akhbâre emruz ro shenidi?	اخبار امروز رو شنیدی؟
You haye a news magazine?	majaleye khabari dâri?	مجله خبری داری؟
I read most of newpapers.	Bishtare ruznâme hâ ro mikhunam.	بیشتر روزنامه ها رو می خونم.
Do you watch TV?	telviziyon mibini?	تلویزیون می بینی؟
This news is not correct!	in khabar sehat nadâre!	این خبر صحت نداره!
I watch BBC channel.	man shabekeye bi bi si negâh mikonam.	من شبکه بی بی سی نگاه می کنم.
I have good news for you.	khabarhâyi khubi barâtun dâram	خبرهای خوبی براتون دارم.
What was happening today?.	emruz che etefâghi oftâde?.	امروز چه اتفاقی افتاده؟
What time is it broadcast?	che zamâni pakhsh mishe?	چه زمانی پخش میشه؟
The news network has not announced anything.	shabakeye khabar hich chizi elâm nakarde.	شبکه خبر هیچ چیزی اعلام نکرده.
Did you see the title of the newspaper?	onvâne ruznâme ro didi?	عنوان روزنامه رو دیدی؟
I read most of the events page.	bishtare safheye havâdes ro khundam.	بیشتر صفحه حوادث رو خوندم.
I want to listen to news.	mikhâm be akhbâr gush bedam.	میخوام به اخبار گوش بدم.

Giving bad news and Responding to Bad News	khabare bad dâdan va javâb dadan be khbare bad.	خبر بد دادن و جواب دادن به خبر بد
English	**Pronunciation**	**Persian**
I'm afraid I've got some bad news for you.	khabarâye badi barâtun dâram.	ببخشید خبرهای بدی براتون دارم.
I'm sorry to have to tell you that …	moteasefam ke bâyad in ro begam.	متاسفم که باید این رو بگم.
I really don't know how to say it.	vâghean nemidunam chetor in ro begam.	واقعاً نمیدونم چطور این رو بگم.
I know this isn't what you want to hear.	midunam in chizi nist ke bekhây beshnavi.	میدونم این چیزی نیست که بخوای بشنوی.
I'm afraid to inform you.	mitarsam behetun etelâ bedam.	میترسم بهتون اطلاع بدم.
I really feel bad to have to say this, but …	vâghean ehsâse badi dâram in ro begam.	واقعاً احساس بدی دارم این رو بگم.
I'm sorry to hear that.	moteasefam in ro mishnavam.	متاسفم این رو می شنوم.
That's awful!	che bad!	چه بد!
Poor!	bichare!	بیچاره!
What a pity!	âkhey!	آخی!
Please accept my sympathy.	lotfan hamdardim ro bepazir.	لطفاً همدردیم رو بپذیر.
there's anything I can do, just let me know.	age chizi hast ke betunam anjâm bedam begu.	اگه چیزی هست که بتونم انجام بدم، بگو.
Too bad!	kheili bade!	خیلی بده!

Describing Personality — توصیف شخصیت — tosife shakhsiyat

English	Pronunciation	Persian
He speaks a lot!	kheili harf mizane!	!خیلی حرف میزنه
My friend behaves like children.	dustam mesle bachehâ raftâr mikone.	.دوستم مثل بچه ها رفتار میکنه
Its gets angry soon.	zud asabâni mishe.	.زود عصبانی میشه
He is talking logically.	un bâ mantegh harf mizane.	.اون با منطق حرف میزنه
His behavior is intimate with me.	raftâresh bâ man samimiye.	.رفتارش با من صمیمیه
My father is very kind.	bâbâm kheili mehrabune.	.بابام خیلی مهربونه
My wife is shy.	khânumam khejâlatiye.	.خانومم خجالتیه
Our manager is very good!	modiremun kheili khube!	!مدیرمون خیلی خوبه
My friend takes a hasty decision!	dustam bâ ajale tasmim migire!	!دوستم با عجله تصمیم میگیره
S/he is very sensitive.	un kheili hasâse.	!اون خیلی حساسه
I became very sensitive.	man kheili hasâs shodam.	.من خیلی حساس شدم
Ali has a good talent.	ali estedâde khubi dâre.	.علی استعداد خوبی داره
My brother gets angry soon.	barâdaram zud asabâni mishe.	.برادرم زود عصبانی میشه
S/he laying a lot!	kheili durugh mige!	!خیلی دروغ میگه
My sister is afrid of the mouse.	khâharam az mush mitarse.	.خواهرم از موش میترسه
S/he talks a little.	kheili kame harf mizane.	.خیلی کم حرف میزنه

آدرس دادن
To Give Address
âdres dâdan

English	Pronunciation	Persian
Which route should I go?	kodum masir bâyad beram?	کدوم مسیر باید برم؟
Go straight, end of the street.	mostaghim boru, entahâye khiyâbun.	مستقیم برو، انتهای خیابون.
It's a few meters ahead.	chand metr jolotare.	چند متر جلوتره.
Can you give me the address?	mituni behem âdres bedi?	میتونی بهم آدرس بدی؟
Tank you for giving me the address.	mamnun râho neshun dâdi.	ممنون راه رو نشون دادی.
Where is the highway exit?	khorujiye bozorgrâh kodum tarafe?	خروجی بزرگراه کدوم طرفه؟
Please show me the road map.	lotfan naghsheye râh ro behem neshun bede.	لطفا نقشه راه رو بهم نشون بده.
The Taxi is over there.	tâksi untaraf hast.	تاکسی اون طرف هست.
Excuse me where is the café?	bebakhshid kâfi shâp kogâst?	ببخشید کافی شاپ کجاست؟
The street is one-way.	khiyabun ye tarefe hast.	خیابون یه طرفه هست.
Which route is closer?	kodum masir nazdiktare?	کدوم مسیر نزدیک تره؟
Sorry, I wanted to ask the address!	bebakhshid mikhâstam âdres beporsam.	ببخشید، میخواستم آدرس بپرسم!
From the right side of the main strees.	az samte râste khiyâbune asli.	از سمت راست خیابون اصلی.
Across the gym.	roberuye bâshgâh.	رو به روی باشگاه.
The bank is on the other side of the street.	bânk unvare khiyâbune.	بانک اون ور خیابونه.
Where is the hospital?	bimârestân kojâst?	بیمارستان کجاست؟
Is the subway station here?	istgâhe metro injast?	ایستگاه مترو اینجاست؟

	خواب	
	Sleep khâb	
English	**Pronunciation**	**Persian**
I lost my nice sleep!	khâbe nâzo az dast dâdam!	!خواب ناز و از دست دادم
I feel sleepy.	khâbam miyâd.	.خوابم میاد
My dream came true.	khâbam tabir shod.	.خوابم تعبیر شد
I sleep here.	man injâ mikhâbam!	.من این جا میخوابم
I wake up early.	man zud bidâr misham.	.من زود بیدار میشم
I could not sleep well last night.	dishab natunestam bekhâbam.	.دیشب نتونستم بخوابم
He is a heavey sleeper!	khâbesh sangine!	!خوابش سنگینه
Go to sleep.	boro bekhâb.	.برو بخواب
I had a terrible nightmare.	khâbe vahshatnâki didam.	.خواب وحشتناکی دیدم
What time do you sleep?	che sâati mikhâbi?	چه ساعتی می خوابی؟
I want to sleep.	mikhâm bekhâbam.	.میخوام بخوابم
I sleep early at night.	shabâ zud mikhâbam.	.شب ها زود میخوابم
How soon he fell asleep!	che zud khâbid!	!چه زود خوابید
Are you asleep or awake?	khâbi yâ bidâr?	خوابی یا بیدار؟
I cannot sleep.	namitunam bekhâbam.	.نمیتونم بخوابم
When did you get up?	key bidâr shodi?	کی بیدار شدی؟
Where do you sleep?	kojâ mikhâbi?	کجا میخوابی؟

Taxi	tâksi	تاکسی
English	**Pronunciation**	**Persian**
Where is a taxi stand?	istgâhe tâksi kojâst?	ایستگاه تاکسی کجاست؟
Where is your rout?	masiretun kojâst?	مسیرتون کجاست؟
Where are you going?	kojâ miri?	کجا میری؟
I want to go to the airport.	mikhâm beram forudgâh.	میخوام برم فرودگاه.
How much is fare?	kerâye chand mishe?	کرایه چند میشه؟
Close the car door.	dare mâshin ro beband.	در ماشین رو ببند.
Go faster, I'm in a hurry!	saritar boro, ajale dâram!	سریع تر برو، عجله دارم!
Please take a direct route.	lotfan aze masire mostaghim boro.	لطفا از مسیر مستقیم برو.
Can you wait?	mituni montazer bemuni?	می تونی منتظر بمونی؟
What's the fare?	kerâye chande?	کرایه چنده؟
Give me the change.	baghiyeye pulam ro bede.	بقیه پولم رو بده.
How much is the fee to the airport.	kerâye tâ forudgâh chande?	کرایه تا فرودگاه چنده؟
How much is it?	cheghadr mishe?	چقدر میشه؟
How long dose it take ?	cheghadr tul mikeshe ?	چقدر طول میکشه؟

Complements		تعریف کردن
		tarif kardan
English	Pronunciation	Persian
Good job!	âfarin!	آفرین!
Well done!	bârikalâ!	باریکلا!
Fantastic!	khieyâlie	خیلی عالیه!
That's great!	âlieye!	عالیه!
Nice work!	kâret khub bud!	کارت خوب بود!
Excellent!	âlieiy!	عالی بود!
Well done!	kâret doroste!	کارت درسته!
Good grades!	che nomreye khubi!	چه نمره خوب!
What a nice dress!	che lebâse khubi.	چه لباس خوبی!
You look great!	âliey be nazar mieyây	عالی به نظر میای!
Your dress is beautiful!	lebâset ghashange!	لباست قشنگه!
You have a good voice!	sedâyi khubi dâri	صدای خوبی داری!
You look awesome!	kheili khoshtip be nazar miyâye.	خیلی خوش تیپ به نظر میای.
I like your haircut.	muhâto dust dâram	موهات رو دوست دارم.
What a beautiful house!	che khuneye ghashangi!	چه خونه قشنگی!
What a nice apartment!	che âpârtemâne khubiye!	چه آپارتمان خوبیه!

Making and Answering A Phone Call

جواب دادن به تلفن
javâb dâdan be telfon

English	Pronunciation	Persian
Hello! (on the phone)	alo	الو
Can I speak with Reza?	mitunam bâ rezâ sohbat konam.	میتونم با رضا صحبت کنم؟
I'd like to speak to Reza.	mikhâm bâ rezâ sohbat konam.	میخوام با رضا صحبت کنم.
Hold the line.	ye lahze gushi!	یه لحظه گوشی!
I'll connect you now.	man alân shomâ ro vasl mikonam.	من الان شما رو وصل میکنم.
I'm sorry, he's not available at the moment.	moteasefam un alân nist.	متاسفم، او الان نیست.
Please call back later.	lotfan badan tamâs begir.	لطفاً بعدا تماس بگیر.
Would you like to leave a message?	mikhây payâm bezâri?	می خوای پیام بذاری؟
Who's speaking?	ki sohbat mikone?	کی صحبت می کنه؟
Could I ask who's calling?	mitunam beporsam ki tamâs migire?	میتونم بپرسم کی تماس میگیره؟
Can I have your name, please?	lotfan mitunam esmetun ro beporsam?	لطفاً میتونم اسمتون رو بپرسم؟
Is it convenient to talk at the moment?	mituni alân sohbat koni?	میتونی الان صحبت کنی؟
Hang on for a moment.	ye lahze sabr kon.	لحظه ای صبر کن.
Could you please speak up?	lotfan mituni sohbat koni?	لطفاً میتونی صحبت کنی؟
Please speak louder.	lotfan bolandtar sohbat kon.	لطفاً بلندتر صحبت کن.
Please stay on the line.	lotfan poshte khat bemun.	لطفاً پشت خط بمون.
I got the wrong number.	man shomâraro eshtebâh gereftam.	من شماره رو اشتباه گرفتم.
I will call again later.	man dobâre zang mizanam	من دوباره زنگ می زنم.

Age سن sen		
English	Pronunciation	Persian
How old are you?	chand salete?	چند سالته؟
How old is she/he?	un chand sâleshe?	اون چند سالشه؟
How old is your son?	persaret chand sâleshe?	پسرت چند سالشه؟
S/he is old.	un pire.	اون پیره.
S/he is so young.	un kheili javune.	اون خیلی جوونه.
S/he seems to be a child.	be nazar bache mirese.	به نظر بچه می رسه.
S/he seems to be at middle age.	be nazar miyânsâle.	به نظر میانساله
S/he seems to be 30 years old.	be nazar si sâle mirese.	به نظر سی ساله می رسه.
I'm twenty one years old.	bisto yek sâlame.	بیست و یک سالمه.
I'm tw years older than you are.	man do sâl azat bozorgtaram.	من دو سال ازت بزرگترم.
Guess how old I am.	hads bezan chand sâlame!	حدس بزن چند سالمه؟
I'm the eldest son of the family.	man pesare bozorge khunevâdeam.	من پسر بزرگ خونواده ام.
May I ask your age?	momkene senet ro beporsam?	ممکنه سنت رو بپرسم؟
I'm younger than you are.	man az shomâ javuntaram.	من از شما جوون ترم.
I'm the youngest.	man kuchektaram.	من کوچکترین هستم.

Promises and Useful Responses
قول دادن و جواب های مفید

ghol dadan va javâb hâye mofid

English	Pronunciation	Persian
I promise.	ghol midam.	قول می دم.
Promise me.	behem ghol bede.	بهم قول بده.
We promise you.	behet ghol midim.	بهت قول میدیم.
S/he promised me.	un behem ghol dâd	اون بهم قول داد.
Keep your promise.	be gholet amal kon.	به قولت عمل کن.
I promise that I will finish this job on time.	ghol midam in kâro be moghe anjâm bedam.	قول میدم این کارو به موقع انجام بدم.
Trust me, I can do it.	behem etemâd kon, mitunam un ro anjâm bedam.	به من اعتماد کن، میتونم اون رو انجام بدم.
S/he doesn't keep her/his promise.	un be gholesh amal nemikone.	اون به قولش عمل نمی کنه.
I swear.	ghasam mikhoram	قسم می خورم.
I assure you.	man behet etminân midam.	من بهت اطمینان می دم.
Trust me.	be man etminân kon.	به من اطمینان کن.
Hop you do it.	omidvâram in kâr ro anjâm bedi.	امیدوارم این کارو انجام بدی.

Speaking in Farsi		صحبت کردن به فارسی
		sohbat kardan be fârsi
English	Pronunciation	Persian
Could you speak up a little, please?	lotfan mituni kami boland sohbat koni?	لطفاً میتونی کمی بلند صحبت کنی؟
Could you please say that again?	lotfan mituni in ro dobâre begi?	لطفاً میتونی دوباره بگی؟
Could you please repeat that?	lotfan mituni un ro tekrâr koni?	لطفاً میتونی اون رو تکرار کنی؟
How do you pronounce this word?	chetor in kalemaro talafoz mikoni?	چطور این کلمه رو تلفظ می کنی؟
What's the meaning of this?	mani in chei mishe?	معنی این چی میشه؟
I'm sorry, what do you mean?	bebakhshid, manzuret chiye?	ببخشید، منظورت چیه؟
What is this thing called in Farsi?	in chiz tu fârsi chi mishe?	این چیز تو فارسی چی می شه؟
How many languages can you speak?	chand zabun mituni sohbat koni?	چند زبون میتونی صحبت می کنی؟
I speak a little Farsi.	mitunam kami fârsi sohbat konam.	میتونم کمی فارسی صحبت کنم.
I don't speak Farsi very well.	man fârsi ro kheili khub sohbat nemikonam.	من فارسی رو خیلی خوب صحبت نمی کنم.
My Farsi is not good.	fârsiye man khub nist.	فارسی من خوب نیست.
I can read Farsi very well, but I can't speak.	man mitunam fârsi ro khub bekhunam, amâ nemitunam sohbat konam.	من میتونم فارسی رو خوب بخونم، اما نمیتونم صحبت کنم.
I would like to improve my Farsi.	mikhâm fârsim ro behtar konam.	میخوام فارسیم رو بهتر کنم.
Your Farsi is excellent.	fârsiye shomâ âliye.	فارسی شما عالیه.

Asking for Opinions

پرسیدن عقاید

porsidane aghâyed

English	Pronunciation	Persian
What do you thing about this problem?	dar mored in moshkel chi fekr mikoni?	در مورد این مشکل چی فکر می کنی؟
Do you have any thoughts on that?	shomâ dar morede un chi fekr mikoni?	شما در مورد اون فکر چی می کنی؟
How do you feel about that?	che hesi dar morede un dâri?	چه حسی در مورد اون داری؟
What is your opinion?	nazaretun chiye?	نظرتون چیه؟
Do you have any idea?	nazari dâri?	نظری داری؟
Do you have any opinion on this matter?	dar morede in mozu' nazari dâri?	در مورد این موضوع نظری داری؟
What's your view?	chi fekr mikoni?	چی فکر می کنی؟
Please say your opinion on this subject?	lotfan nazaretun ro dar morede in mozu' begin.	لطفاً نظرتون رو در مورد این موضوع بگین.
Can I ask your opinion?	mitunam nazaretun ro beporsam?	میتونم نظرتون رو بپرسم؟
What is your opinion about that?	nazaretun dar mored in chiye?	نظرتون در مورد این چیه؟
What are you feeling about that?	dar morede un che hesi dâri?	در مورد او چه حسی داری؟

Hope and Disappointment		امیدواری و نا امیدی
		omidâri va nâomidi
English	Pronunciation	Persian
I became disappointed.	kheili nâomid shodam.	خیلی ناامید شدم.
I don't know what to do.	nemidunam chikâr konam.	نمی دونم چیکار کنم.
I hope to see you soon.	omidvâram be zudi bebinamet.	امیدوارم به زودی ببینمت.
I hope he will get better.	omidvâram un behtar beshe.	امیدوارم اون بهتر بشه.
Hopefully it'll be sunny tomorrow.	omidvâram fardâ âftabi beshe.	امیدوارم فردا آفتابی بشه.
Do not lose your hope.	omidet ro az dast nade.	امیدت رو از دست نده.
I hope everything goes well.	omidvâram hame chiz khub pish bere.	امیدوارم همه چیز خوب پیش بره.
I wish it would stop raining.	arezu mikonam barun band biyâd.	آرزو می کنم بارون بند بیاد.
Never be disappointed.	hargez nâomid nasho.	هرگز ناامید نشو.
I'm discouraged.	man delsardam.	من دلسردم.
I don't have any hope.	omid nadâram.	امید ندارم.
I have no motivation.	man angize'i nadârm.	من انگیزه ای ندارم.

Health and Illness

سلامتی و مریضی

salâmati va marizi

English	Pronunciation	Persian
What's the problem?	moshkelet chiye?	مشکلت چیه؟
What are your symptoms?	alâeme marizit chiye?	علائم مریضیت چیه؟
Are you feeling any better?	behtar nashodi?	بهتر نشدی؟
Do you have any allergies?	âlerzhi dâri?	آلرژی داری؟
How long have you been feeling like this?	az kei dard dâri?	از کی درد داری؟
Do you have any medicine to take?	ghors mikhori?	قرصی می خوری؟
How do you feed today?	hâlet emruz chetore?	حالت امروز چطوره؟
Are you sick?	marizi?	مریضی؟
Don't you feed well?	hâlet khub nist?	حالت خوب نیست؟
Where does it pain?	kojât dard mikone?	کجات درد می کنه؟
Do you feel any pain?	jâyit dard mikone?	جاییت درد می کنه؟
From when do you feel pain?	az key dard mikone?	از کی درد داری؟
I have a fever.	man tab dâram	من تب دارم.
I have a headache.	saram dard mikone	سرم درد می کنه.
I have a back pain.	kamaram dard mikone	کمرم درد می کنه.
I have a toothache.	dandunam dard mikone	دندونم درد می کنه.
I have a stomach ache.	me'dam dard mikone	معده ام درد می کنه.
I've got a slight headache.	man kami sardard dâram.	من کمی سردرد دارم.
I've got a sore throat.	galum dard mikone.	گلوم درد می کنه.
I have a high blood pressure.	feshâre khun dâram.	فشار خون دارم.

Shopping	khardi	خرید
English	Pronunciation	Persian
Where is the shopping area?	mantagheye kharid kojâst?	منطقه خرید کجاست؟
Where is the nearest bookstore?	nazdiktarin ketâb forushi kojâst?	نزدیکترین کتاب فروشی کجاست؟
Where is the nearest ATM?	Nazdiktarin ei tie m kojâst?	نزدیکترین ای تی ام کجاست؟
Where is the nearest shoe store?	nazdiktarin maghâzeye kafsh forushi kojâst?	نزدیکترن مغازه کفش فروشی کجاست؟
Where is the nearest clothing store?	nazdiktarin forushgâhe pushâk kojast?	نزدیکترین فروشگاه پوشاک کجاست؟
Where is the nearest market?	nazdiktarin bâzâr kojâst?	نزدیکترین بازار کجاست؟
Where is the nearest drugstore?	nazdiktarin dârukhâne kojâst?	نزدیکترین داروخونه کجاست؟
I would like to try it on.	mikhâm in ro poro konam	می خوام این رو پرو کنم.
I would like a suit.	man ye dast koto shalvâre mikhâm.	من یه دست کت و شلوار می خوام.
Where's the fitting room?	otâghe poro kojâst?	اتاق پرو کجاست؟
It doesn't quite fit me.	kâmelan andâzeye man nist	کاملاً اندازه من نیست.
It's too short.	kheyli kutâhe	خیلی کوتاهه
It's too long.	kheyli bolande	خیلی بلنده
It's too tight.	kheyli tange	خیلی تنگه
It's too loose.	kheyli goshâde	خیلی گشاده
I want to buy a battery.	man mikhâm ye bâtri bekharam	من می خوام یه باتری بخرم.
Have you got any flashlight batteries?	bâtriye cherâgh ghove dârid?	باتری چراغ قوه دارید؟
I would like a ring.	man ye angoshtar mikhâm	من یه انگشتر می خوام.
I would like to have a couple bulbs	man chand tâ lâmp mikhâm	من چند تا لامپ می خوام.

Booking		رزرو کردن
		rezerv kardan
English	Pronunciation	Persian
What's the problem?	moshkelet chiye?	مشکلت چیه؟
What are your symptoms?	alâeme marizit chiye?	علائم مریضیت چیه؟
Are you feeling any better?	behtar nashodi?	بهتر نشدی؟
Do you have any allergies?	âlerzhi dâri?	آلرژی داری؟
How long have you been feeling like this?	az kei dard dâri?	از کی درد داری؟
Do you have any medicine to take?	ghors mikhori?	قرصی می خوری؟
How do you feed today?	hâlet emruz chetore?	حالت امروز چطوره؟
Are you sick?	marizi?	مریضی؟
Don't you feed well?	hâlet khub nist?	حالت خوب نیست؟
Where does it pain?	kojât dard mikone?	کجات درد می کنه؟
Do you feel any pain?	jâyit dard mikone?	جاییت درد می کنه؟
From when do you feel pain?	az key dard mikone?	از کی درد داری؟
I have a fever.	man tab dâram	من تب دارم.
I have a headache.	saram dard mikone	سرم درد می کنه.
I have a back pain.	kamaram dard mikone	کمرم درد می کنه.
I have a toothache.	dandunam dard mikone	دندونم درد می کنه.
I have a stomach ache.	me'dam dard mikone	معده ام درد می کنه.
I've got a slight headache.	man kami sardard dâram.	من کمی سردرد دارم.
I've got a sore throat.	galum dard mikone.	گلوم درد می کنه.
I have a high blood pressure.	feshâre khun dâram.	فشار خون دارم.

Other Books of Interest

Learn Farsi in 100 Days

The Ultimate Crash Course to Learning Farsi Fast

The goal of this book is simple. It will help you incorporate the best method and the right strategies to learn Farsi FAST and EFFECTIVELY.

Learn Farsi in 100 days helps you learn speak Farsi faster than you ever thought possible. You only need to spend about 90-120 minutes daily in your 100-day period in order to learn Farsi language at advanced level. Whether you are just starting to get in touch the Farsi language, or even if you have already learned the basics of the language, this book can help you accelerate the learning process and put you on the right track.

Learn Farsi in 100 days is for Farsi learners from the beginning to the advanced level. It is a breakthrough in Farsi language learning — offering a winning formula and the most powerful methods for learning to speak Farsi fluently and confidently. Each contains 4 pages covering a comprehensive range of topics. Each day includes vocabulary, grammar, reading and writing lessons. It gives learners easy access to the Farsi vocabulary and grammar as it is actually used in a comprehensive range of everyday life situations and it teaches students to use Farsi for situations related to work, social life, and leisure. Topics such as greetings, family, weather, sports, food, customs, etc. are presented in interesting unique ways using real-life information.

Purchase on Amazon website:

https://goo.gl/eG2n11

Published By:
LearnPersianOnline.com

Farsi Conversations
Learn the Most Common Words and Phrases Farsi Speakers use Every Day

Learning about a new culture is always an exciting prospect and one of the best ways to get to know about another country, its people and their customs, is to learn the language.

Now, with Farsi Conversations: Learn the Most Common Words and Phrases Farsi Speakers use Every Day you can learn how to communicate in Farsi and learn more about Persian culture at the same time.

In this unique guide, you will be able to practice your spoken Farsi with FREE YouTube videos. It is an ideal tool for learners of Farsi at all levels, whether at school, in evening classes or at home, and is a 'must have' for business or leisure.

Farsi students can learn;

- How to use the right language structures and idioms in the right context
- Practice Farsi vocabulary and phrases needed in everyday situations
- Gain proficiency in written and spoken Farsi
- New ways of mastering Farsi phrases

By the end of the book you will have learned more than 2500 Farsi words, have mastered more than 300 commonly used Farsi verbs, key expressions and phrases and be able to pose more than 800 questions.

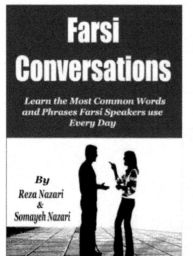

Purchase on Amazon website:

https://goo.gl/bGpVNZ

Published By:
LearnPersianOnline.com

100 Most Popular Persian Songs

Music is a vital part of Persian culture and Persians love music. Listening to Persian songs and reading the lyrics along with the song is not only a good way to improve your Persian but the best way to learn about Persian culture and enjoy it.

Songs always contain a lot of valuable vocabulary, phrases and expressions. Most popular songs have many repeated phrases which, once you've learned to sing the song, can be immediately put to use in conversation.

100 Most Memorable Persian Songs of All Time offers the lyrics of the most popular Persian songs, ranked by ManoTo TV Channel.

Most Popular Farsi Idioms

Idioms with Their English Equivalents

This handy book is a collection of 300 most popular Farsi idioms used in everyday context with their best equivalents in English. The idioms provided here can help the keen learner broaden their knowledge of the Farsi language and culture.

Farsi speaking natives love to use idioms. The Essential idioms in this book offer an additional look at the idiomatic phrases and sayings that make Farsi the rich language that it is.

A compilation of 300 most popular Farsi idioms widely used in Iran in everyday context with their best English equivalents are presented with illustrations so that learners using this section will have many idioms 'at their fingertips'.

LearnPersianOnline.com

Funny Persian Stories

Mulla Nasreddin Tales

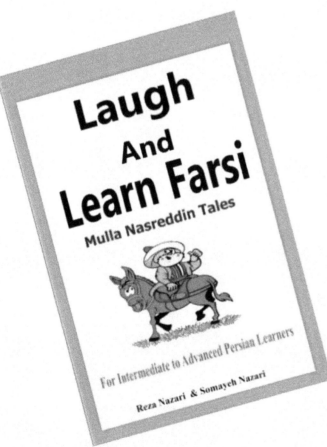

Mullah Nasreddin is a famous Persian character who appears in many funny Persian stories. He is always humorous, wise, and sometimes philosophic. Mulla's stories are generally funny, but in the subtle humor there is always a lesson to be learned.

Just hearing Molla's name brings smile to Persians. You cannot find an Iranian who does not know a few stories of Mulla.

This book offers about 200 funny stories of
Mulla Nasreddin

The only Farsi Grammar Book You'll Ever Need!

Farsi Grammar in Use is a series of three volumes.

This volume is for students at intermediate level.

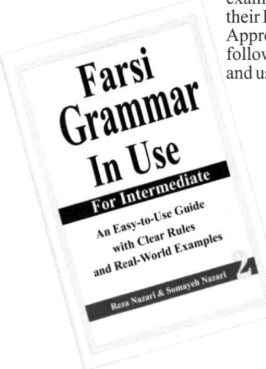

Farsi Grammar in Use is an entertaining guide to Farsi grammar and usage.
This user-friendly resource includes simple explanations of grammar and useful examples to help students of all ages improve their Farsi.
Appropriate for any age range, this easy-to-follow guide makes learning Farsi grammar and usage simple and fun.

For anyone who wants to understand the major rules and subtle guidelines of Farsi grammar and usage, Farsi Grammar in Use offers comprehensive, straightforward instruction. It covers a wide range of subjects as they are taught in many language schools around the world.

Farsi Grammar in Use is written for students who find the subjects unusually difficult and confusing -or in many cases, just plain boring. It doesn't take a lifetime to master Farsi grammar. All it takes is Farsi Grammar in Use. Filled with clear examples and self-assessment quizzes, this is one of the most highly trusted Farsi language resources available.

LearnPersianOnline.com

Greatest Persian poets

Greatest Persian poets as Rumi, Hafez and Saadi, and their most beautiful

Persian is a naturally lovely, elegant and romantic language and poetry is an essential piece of it.

For centuries, the world's most influential and inspiring poets, whose works attracted many people in the world, have been living in the Persian-speaking countries.

Therefore, Persian poetry is a unique breed. It's full of life, love, and romantic phrases and everything beyond.

his book can be useful for students and enjoyable for poetry lovers of any age. Not only will poems improve your Persian language, but they'll help your understanding of Persian culture.

LearnPersianOnline.com

Easy Persian Phrasebook

Essential Expressions for Communicating in Persian

Designed as a quick reference and study guide, this comprehensive phrasebook offers guidance for situations including traveling, accommodations, healthcare, emergencies and other common circumstances. A phonetic pronunciation accompanies each phrase and word.

Easy Persian Phrasebook is designed to teach the essentials of Persian quickly and effectively. The common words and phrases are organized to enable the reader to handle day to day situations. The book should suit anyone who needs to get to grips quickly with Persian, such as tourists and business travelers.

The book "*Easy Persian Phrasebook*" is incredibly useful for those who want to learn Persian language quickly and efficiently.

You'll be surprised how fast you master the first steps in learning Persian, this beautiful language!

Purchase on Amazon website:

   https://goo.gl/d21Ivg

Published By:

LearnPersianOnline.com

Top 1,500 Persian Words

Essential Words for Communicating in Persian

Designed as a quick reference and study guide, this reference book provides easy-to-learn lists of the most relevant Persian vocabulary. Arranged by 36 categories, these word lists furnish the reader with an invaluable knowledge of fundamental vocabulary to comprehend, read, write and speak Persian.

Top 1,500 Persian Words is intended to teach the essentials of Persian quickly and effectively. The common words are organized to enable the reader to handle day-to-day situations. Words are arranged by topic, such as Family, Jobs, weather, numbers, countries, sports, common verbs, etc. A phonetic pronunciation accompanies each word.

With daily practice, you can soon have a working vocabulary in Persian!

The book "*Top 1,500 Persian Words*" is incredibly useful for those who want to learn Persian language **quickly** and **efficiently.**

Learn Most Common Persian Words FAST!

Purchase on Amazon website:

https://goo.gl/YvhpKe

Published By:
LearnPersianOnline.com

Farsi Reading

Improve your reading skill and discover the art, culture and history of Iran:

Organized by specific reading skills, this book is designed to enhance students' Farsi reading. The entertaining topics motivate students to learn. Lively reading passages present high-interest subjects for most Farsi speakers. The short essays deepen student knowledge while strengthening reading skills.

Fifty articles in this books representing a diversity of interests intended to develop topics of central interest to Farsi language, culture, and society. Each of the book's topics is a simple essay about Iran's language, geography, culture and history.

Purchase on Amazon website:

https://goo.gl/Fe5O0t   https://goo.gl/HBcNiV   https://goo.gl/U8UxMm

Published By:
LearnPersianOnline.com

100 Jokes in Farsi

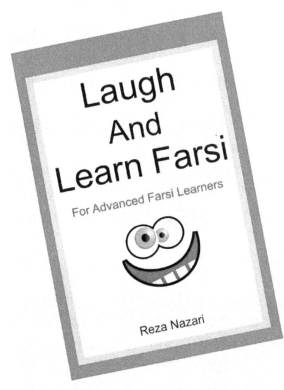

Laugh and learn Farsi is a supplementary text for advanced students and professionals who want to better understand Farsi native speakers, publications and media.

It's especially for those who have learned Farsi outside of Iran. If you already speak Farsi, but now would like to start speaking even better, then this book is just for you.

If you really want to understand Farsi Language, you need to understand the jokes that people tell in Farsi! Check out the 100 jokes in this book and see if you understand them. Try telling a joke you like to your friends. It's a good way to practice your Farsi.

If you really want to understand Farsi Language, you need to understand the jokes that people tell in Farsi!

LearnPersianOnline.com

100 Fun, Interesting, and Appealing Short Stories

If you're learning Persian and love reading, this is the book you need to take your Persian to the next level

LearnPersianOnline.com

Designed for Persian lovers at the intermediate and advanced level, this book offers 100 fun, interesting, and appealing short stories. The stories motivate you to enjoy reading enthusiastically.

100 Short Stories in Persian contains simple yet entertaining stories to help you improve your Persian reading and writing skills by covering a diverse range of grammar structures and vocabulary.

Reading short stories is probably the best way for most Persian lovers to improve their Persian conveniently.

This book comes with a Persian and English glossary, so you can find the meaning of keywords in stories. Get this book now and start learning Persian the fun way!

   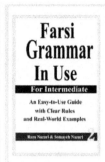 

"learn Persian Online" Publications

Learn Persian Online authors' team strives to prepare and publish the best quality Persian Language learning resources to make learning Persian easier for all. We hope that our publications help you learn this lovely language in an effective way.

Please let us know how your studies turn out. We would like to know what part of our books worked for you and how we can make these books better for others. You can reach us via email at info@learnpersianonline.com

We all in Learn Persian Online wish you good luck and successful studies!

Learn Persian Online Authors

Best Persian Learning Books

Published By:
LearnPersianOnline.com

 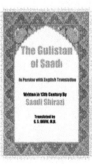 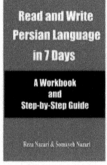  

Learn to Speak Persian Online

Enjoy interactive Persian lessons on Skype with the best native speaking Persian teachers

Online Persian Learning that's Effective, Affordable, Flexible, and Fun.

Learn Persian wherever you want; when you want

Ultimate flexibility. You can now learn Persian online via Skype, enjoy high quality engaging lessons no matter where in the world you are. It's affordable too.

Learn Persian With One-on-One Classes

We provide one-on-one Persian language tutoring online, via Skype. We believe that one-to-one tutoring is the most effective way to learn Persian.

Qualified Native Persian Tutors

Working with the best Persian tutors in the world is the key to success! Our Persian tutors give you the support & motivation you need to succeed with a personal touch.

It's easy! Here's how it works

Request a FREE introductory session
Meet a Persian tutor online via Skype
Start speaking Real Persian in Minutes

Send Email to: info@LearnPersianOnline.com

Or Call: + 1-469-230-3605